ISBN: 978-1-9194203-0-1 (hardcover)

ISBN: 978-1-9194203-1-8 (paperback)

ISBN: 978-1-9194203-2-5 (Kindle)

For enquiries regarding permissions, please contact:

eCom Profits Lab ®

www.ecomprofitslab.com

www.theannadavidson.com

Email: support@theannadavidson.com

Disclaimer

This book is intended for informational, educational, and inspirational purposes only. It does not constitute professional, legal, medical, or psychological advice. The Anna Davidson Ltd disclaims any liability for any errors, omissions, or consequences arising from the use or interpretation of the content. Readers should seek appropriate guidance where necessary.

By engaging with this book, readers acknowledge and accept that The Anna Davidson Ltd and any affiliated parties are not responsible for any claims, disputes, or legal matters arising from the author.

Book cover by www.RushfirthCreative.co.uk

THINK YOU CAN'T SELL ON AMAZON?

(THINK AGAIN) I'LL SHOW YOU HOW

ANNA DAVIDSON

DEDICATION

To my sons Jacob and Reuben, who first and foremost inspire me every day to make impact, my mum, dad and family, friends, and clients for empowering and supporting me to make this book happen.

WHAT OTHERS ARE SAYING

'Anna is a force of nature; not only what she has built but how she has built it. This book maps out exactly what you need to do to completely change your life with an eCommerce or Amazon-based business. Anna walks her talk. Read this book and apply the lessons; you're in safe hands.'

Dan Meredith

International Bestselling Author, Coach and Speaker

'I've had the pleasure of working closely with Anna for a number of years, and I've seen firsthand the integrity, strategy, and heart she brings to everything she does. As an expert within my community of business owners, I only ever recommend people I truly trust and Anna is someone I confidently recommend again and again. Her knowledge of eCommerce and Amazon is matched only by her ability to actually teach it in a clear, actionable way. If she's guiding you, you're being led by someone who genuinely knows the path and has walked it herself. This book is a must-read for anyone wanting to succeed in eCommerce.'

Emma Cooper

Online Business Coach & Agency Owner

'Working with Anna Davidson has been an absolute game changer. We genuinely could not have launched on Amazon without her expertise, guidance, and the way she consistently overdelivers in everything she does. Anna makes the entire process simple, strategic, and stress-free, and the value she provides is on another level. If you've got her book in your hands, read it, highlight it, implement every word. You will not be disappointed. Anna is the real deal.'

Jess Crane

Founder, SheEO Collective ®

TABLE OF CONTENTS

PREFACE

Before I get into the meat and potatoes of this book and why you should listen to me, I want to share some of my personal story as this part of my story was the reason I changed my trajectory and also the fuel to my success. Warning though, as this might be a bit heavy and intense for some, but it's my truth and I want you to understand that whatever personal circumstances you are in, you can change.

It was my birthday, and I found myself lying motionless on the bedroom floor. This time, I didn't even try to stand up. I was trapped beneath the mattress that had been flipped over on top of me. Something inside me knew things could not go on this way. I had whispered this to myself before, but every time I gathered the courage, he twisted the story until I believed I was the one to blame, and I stayed. Each cycle grew stranger and darker; clothes and wedding photographs burned, accusations that I was somehow the devil. I kept asking myself what had happened to the man I loved, the man I thought I would grow old with. I fought desperately to hold onto the picture of us, to keep the marriage alive.

We had vowed to love each other in sickness and in health, and I had convinced myself that meant enduring the chaos. Everyone has hard times, I reasoned. If he had been diagnosed with cancer, I wouldn't walk away, I would fight for him. But this was different. It kept happening. I had tried to get him help, but nothing changed.

My marriage was gone. Shattered. The only thing I was certain of was that I needed to get myself and my boys out safely. They had witnessed enough. It felt like it took me forever to finally break free, and I carried so much guilt. What would my, and his, parents think?

The truth was simple: this was abuse, manipulative and dangerous. And I could no longer pretend I could save him. I had become the target, and for the sake of my own sanity and my children's future, I had to go. Staying meant teaching my boys a warped version of love, one that I could not allow to take root in them.

Let me make this clear: I'm not anti-men. I love men, and let's face it, I was bringing up two sons I wanted to inspire. I was surrounded by men in my corporate career, I loved the ambitious, driven male energy I was amongst, and my dad has always been a great role model to me.

From the outside, people thought I had it all. I'd spent sixteen years in the corporate world, well known as the 'Viagra rep,' driving the company car, collecting bonuses, living in the nice house. By appearances, I had 'made it.' But behind closed doors, my life was unravelling. And deep down, I knew I didn't just need to leave the marriage. I needed to leave that career too. The work no longer fulfilled me. My freedom was limited, my income capped, and I hated being pulled away from my boys when they were so little. I always had an entrepreneurial spark, a hunger for something meaningful, but after the collapse of my marriage my self-belief was shattered. I couldn't see where to begin.

There were moments I felt like giving up completely. But then, a quiet voice inside urged me to rise, to use my pain to help others who had walked a similar path. If I could listen, if I could act, it might transform everything. Still, doubt consumed me. Who would take me seriously? I had no formal qualifications in this stuff, no training, my cash flow had been affected after being made redundant. My confidence was at rock bottom. So I hesitated, and I held back.

I found myself late at night endlessly typing searches into Google, everything from 'how to save your marriage' to 'ways to make money online.' I was desperate for answers, desperate for change. Somewhere in that search, I then invested in a digital marketing programme. It was my first real step into the online world. Looking back, I realise just how much I've poured into self-development over the years. Not every investment paid off, some were frankly disappointing, but overall it's been worth it. Every course, every piece of knowledge shaped me in some way. I believe our mindset is everything.

I started applying what I learned, then running small consultancy projects on Facebook marketing. I had become skilled at paid ads, and it was clear to me that small businesses were hungry for help in attracting more customers online. That was my entry point, but it was never the end goal.

Then one day, almost by chance, I stumbled onto a webinar titled 'How to Sell on Amazon.'

At first, I wasn't sure what to expect. I'd always been curious about eCommerce, but the idea of building an actual business on Amazon seemed almost unreal, like something 'other people' did. But as I listened, something clicked. For the first time in a long time, I felt a spark of possibility. This wasn't just theory, it was practical. It was a system I could learn, apply, and grow with.

I remember closing my laptop that night and feeling this mix of fear and excitement. Could I really do this? Could I build something new from scratch? Part of me doubted it, whispered, 'You've already failed once, you're not cut out for this.'But a stronger part, the voice that had survived so much, told me: 'This could change everything.'

So, I made the decision. I signed up.

The first steps were messy and overwhelming. Learning product research, understanding suppliers, figuring out shipping, dealing with all the jargon. I was scared of making mistakes, and truthfully, I did make plenty. But I also felt alive. Every late night researching products, every spreadsheet, every conversation with a supplier, it was building towards something I could finally call my own.

When I finally launched my very first product, a prenatal vitamin, it wasn't perfect, but it was mine. And when that first sale came through, even if it was just a few pounds, I felt something shift. It was proof. Proof that I could take back control, that I could create a new path for myself and for my boys. That tiny notification lit a fire in me, and I knew there was no turning back.

This was only the start.

The start to me building multiple six and seven-figure brands on platforms like Amazon, Etsy, and TikTok, and through my coaching programmes helping over 3,000 students build profitable businesses, ranging from side hustles earning an extra £500 a month to full-scale eCommerce brands.

In 2020, I was featured in Forbes Magazine and won DHGate's Her Power Entrepreneurship Competition, a prestigious award recognising female business leadership.

THINK YOU CAN'T SELL ON AMAZON?

(THINK AGAIN) I'LL SHOW YOU HOW

In 2013, I was at rock bottom, and in just a few years things completely changed for me. And it can for you too.

This book is for anyone wanting to start a physical product business on Amazon, and whether you have tried before and failed, listened to the 'Gurus' promising to get rich quick, this book is for you. The truth of the matter is that a lot of people fail when selling products online and can't sell on Amazon, but I'm going to show you how.

INTRODUCTION

So... you think you can't sell on Amazon? Let's change that.

You wake up whenever you want.

You take your time pouring that first cup of coffee, no mad dash to get out the door, no checking emails before you've even had a sip. You sit down, breathe, and glance at your phone. Not to scroll through social media, but to check the real notifications that matter.

Sales.

Actual orders.

From people buying products that you created, listed, and launched.

That little buzz, that sweet, satisfying 'cha-ching,' it never gets old.

Sounds good, right?

It's not a pipe dream. This is the daily reality of thousands of online sellers like me. And if you're holding this book, something inside you is ready for a piece of that life too. You're ready for more freedom, more purpose, more you.

Maybe the idea of starting an online business feels exciting, or maybe it feels terrifying. Either way, you're here, and that means something.

Let me ask you straight: are you ready to unlock the secrets of online selling and build your own online business?

If the answer is yes, fantastic. You're in exactly the right place. Let's dive in, and I'll walk with you every step of the way as you start your Amazon journey.

And if you're not quite sure, if the idea feels overwhelming or too far outside your comfort zone, that's okay too. You don't need to know everything right now. You just need to be open to learning. That's what this book is for. I've written it so that no matter where you're starting from, you'll walk away with clarity, confidence, and a practical game plan.

Because here's the truth: if you've ever dreamed of being your own boss, setting your own hours, and building something meaningful from your kitchen table, your sofa, or your tiny home office, then online selling might be exactly what you've been looking for.

Whether you're a creative type who loves crafting, someone who's amazing at spotting great products, or you've got a burning desire to share something with the world, you don't need to be a marketing guru or a tech genius. You just need the right roadmap. That's what this book is about.

For the last ten years, I've had the privilege of coaching thousands of people, and last time I counted it was 3,122, through this journey. I've seen stay-at-home parents create full-time income. I've seen side hustlers grow into brand owners. I've seen people who thought they'd never get out of debt finally experience financial peace, not because they got lucky, but because they got smart and intentional.

I've also seen where most people get stuck

Too many books and courses skim over the real stuff. They don't teach you the practical tools. They confuse you with jargon. Or worse, they sell you the dream of 'get rich quick and leave you feeling like a failure when it doesn't work out that way.

That's not what I'm about. I'm not going to hype you up and then leave you hanging. I've built this book to be your honest, no-fluff, step-by-step companion through the wild and wonderful world of eCommerce.

But before we go any further, let me be real with you.

My journey didn't start from a place of confidence. It started from a place of survival. I was in the thick of a toxic, emotionally abusive marriage. On the floor. Literally. On my birthday, I lay there under a flipped mattress, wondering how I got to that point and how I could possibly climb out. That moment became a turning point. It was the day I realised things had to change. Not someday. Not when the timing was right. Now.

I left. I took my boys. I left the relationship. Eventually, I left the corporate world too, the one that looked shiny on the outside but drained me every day. I wanted more for them, and for me.

But I didn't have it all figured out. I had doubts, fears, and very little direction. I spent so many late nights Googling things like 'how to make money online' and 'how to start a business with no money.'I didn't know where to begin, but I knew I had to begin somewhere.

And that 'somewhere' was Amazon.

It started with one product, a prenatal vitamin, and one sale. Just one. That single order gave me something I hadn't felt in a long time: hope. It was proof that I wasn't stuck. That I wasn't broken. That I could take control of my future, one small step at a time.

Since then, I've launched multiple six and seven-figure product brands across Amazon, Etsy, and even TikTok. I've coached over 3,000 students. I've been featured in Forbes, won awards, and, more importantly, I've built a life where I call the shots. And I want the same for you.

That's why I wrote this book.

We'll start with Amazon, because it's one of the biggest and most powerful platforms in the world, but what you'll learn here will serve you no matter where your journey takes you. You'll learn how to choose a product that sells, how to list it the right way, how to market it, how to price it, and how to avoid the biggest mistakes most beginners make. And most importantly, you'll learn how to build a business, not just a one-time hustle.

You'll get honest strategies, real examples, and encouragement when you hit the inevitable bumps along the road. I'll be with you the whole way.

Another thing, if you're a skim reader (just like me haha), then in each chapter you can skip to the end to see the action points and summary. I've done this so that even if you hate reading, you can still get all the value and takeaway points.

So, are you ready? Not ready to be perfect. Not ready to know everything.

Just ready to start. Ready to believe, even just a little, that your life can look different.

Ready to say yes to something that could completely transform your future.

If you are...

Let's go.

PART 1: BUILDING YOUR ONLINE SELLING FOUNDATION

CHAPTER 1:

WELCOME TO THE WORLD OF ONLINE SELLING

Let me paint a picture for you.

It's one of those grey, drizzly Saturday mornings. The kind where the rain taps against the window and the thought of putting on real clothes, grabbing your keys, and braving the cold feels like far too much effort. But there's that book you've been meaning to buy, the one everyone at work has been raving about, the one all over social media.

In another time, you might have sighed, put on your coat, and dragged yourself into town to find it. But not today. Today, you simply reach for your phone. A couple of taps, a swipe, and before you've even finished your cup of coffee, the order is confirmed. That book is already on its way to your doorstep. You didn't even have to leave the sofa.

That, right there, is the magic of eCommerce. It's seamless.

Effortless. Almost invisible. We hardly think twice about it anymore, yet it's completely transformed the way we live, shop, and even dream.

But here's the twist: this book you're holding isn't about buying things online.

It's about selling them.

Because every time someone, maybe you, maybe me, maybe your neighbour down the street, clicks that little 'Buy Now'button, something much bigger is happening on the other side. There's someone who made that sale possible. Someone who listed that product, wrote that description, uploaded those photos, set that price, and put themselves out there.

And here's the surprising truth: that 'someone'isn't always a global brand or a boardroom full of executives. More often than you'd think, it's a stay-at-home parent who wanted more flexibility, or a student testing a side hustle. It could be a retiree looking for a new project, an artist finally finding a way to make money from their creativity, or an everyday person, someone just like you who decided to take a shot.

Sometimes it's a single laptop on a kitchen table, paired with a head full of ideas and a determination to try. Sometimes it's nothing more than one product, one vision, and one brave step forward.

And here's the most important part:

That 'someone'could absolutely be you.

WHY SELLING ONLINE IS CHANGING LIVES

Online selling isn't just a passing trend. It's a movement. A revolution. It is transforming lives, creating freedom, and putting power back into the hands of everyday people.

Think about the world just a generation ago. If you wanted to start a business, you needed a physical storefront, stock to fill it, staff to help you run it, advertising to get customers through the door, and often tens of thousands of pounds just to get started. Today, the rules have changed completely. Now you can launch a business from your living room, your kitchen table, or even a café with nothing more than a laptop and a decent Wi-Fi connection. That kind of accessibility has rewritten what it means to be an entrepreneur.

I've personally witnessed this transformation time and time again. I've seen mums who were desperate to stay home with their children build small online shops that grew into six-figure businesses. I've seen students who started side hustles turn them into reliable passive income streams that paid for their education. I've seen retirees, who once worried about living on fixed pensions, create thriving online businesses that not only brought in money but also reignited their passions.

This is why online selling is so powerful. It's not about chasing the latest trend or copying what everyone else is doing. It's about creating choice in your life. It's about reclaiming ownership of your income, your time, and your future.

And if the personal stories aren't convincing enough, the numbers certainly are. In 2024, global eCommerce sales topped $6.3 trillion, and projections show that by 2027 that figure will climb to nearly $8 trillion (Statista). In the UK alone, more than 80% of adults shop online on a regular basis, millions of customers browsing and buying every single day. Amazon remains a dominant force in the United States, capturing nearly 40% of all online retail sales. Mobile commerce has surged ahead, now accounting for more than 60% of global purchases. People are literally buying products while they're sitting on the sofa, waiting for a train, or scrolling on their phones during a coffee break.

The way the world shops has changed forever, and that shift has opened the door to enormous opportunities. The only question is: will you step through it?

Common Myths vs Truths About Online Selling

Before I dive in further, let's clear the air. There are so many myths that stop people from even trying. Let's bust a few right now.

Myth 1: You need a lot of money to start.

Truth: *Many sellers start with a few hundred pounds. Platforms like Etsy, eBay, and print-on-demand services let you start lean. Amazon's FBA model allows you to scale without owning a warehouse.*

Myth 2: It's too late, the market is saturated.

Truth: *eCommerce is growing every year. Yes, competition is strong, but new niches open daily. Customers are always looking for new solutions, better designs, and fresh brands.*

Myth 3: You have to be super tech-savvy.

Truth: *If you can use social media, you can learn to sell online. Platforms like Shopify and Amazon Seller Central are built to be user friendly.*

Myth 4: It's passive income from day one.

Truth: *Building your store takes effort upfront: research, setup, and marketing. Passive income comes later, once systems are in place.*

Myth 5: Only big businesses succeed.

Truth: *Some of the most successful sellers are individuals or small teams. They win not by being the biggest, but by being focused, creative, and consistent.*

The Many Places You Can Sell (Amazon Is Just One of Them!)

Most people immediately think of Amazon when they hear 'online selling,' and with good reason. Amazon is a giant, with hundreds of millions of loyal customers. But it's just one piece of the puzzle.

Here's a deeper look at the main platforms:

Amazon

Pros: *Massive audience, built-in trust, Fulfilment by Amazon (FBA) handles storage, shipping, and customer service.*

Cons: *High competition, fees can eat into margins, strict seller policies.*

Best For: *Businesses seeking growth, private-label sellers, and those who want global reach.*

Etsy

Pros: *Perfect for handmade, vintage, crafts, and creative products. Customers love authenticity.*

Cons: *More niche-focused, harder to scale high-volume products, fees per sale.*

Best For: *Artists, jewellery makers, digital download creators.*

eBay

Pros: Great for auctions, collectibles, electronics, or reselling. Quick to start.

Cons: *Lower margins, lots of bargain hunters, competition.*

Best For: *Resellers, flipping enthusiasts, and sellers of second-hand goods.*

Shopify

Pros: *Full control of your brand. Your own store, your own rules. Extremely scalable.*

Cons: *No built-in traffic; you're responsible for marketing.*

Best For: *Entrepreneurs who want to build a brand outside marketplaces.*

TikTok Shop

Pros: *Viral reach, direct audience connection.*

Cons: *Still new, content-driven.*

Best For: *Trend products and video-friendly creators.*

Print-on-Demand

Pros: *No inventory. Products are made to order. Easy to launch.*

Cons: *Lower margins, reliant on platform visibility.*

Best For: *Designers, creatives, and those who want to monetise artwork.*

Kindle Direct Publishing (KDP)

Pros: *Global distribution for books, passive income once published.*

Cons: *Highly competitive, requires marketing effort.*

Best For: *Writers, coaches, and educators.*

Each platform has its strengths. The question isn't 'Which is best?' but 'Which is best for you?'

WHY ONLINE SELLING IS THE WAY FORWARD

Beyond the money, let's talk about why this path is so addictive.

One of the biggest reasons is how accessible it is compared to traditional business. You don't need a huge bank loan, a physical storefront, or a team of employees to get started. With online selling, you can launch with just a fraction of the costs that used to hold people back. That's why so many everyday people, mums, students, side hustlers, and retirees are now turning their ideas into income streams. The barrier to entry has never been lower, and that makes the opportunity incredibly exciting.

But it's not just about low start-up costs; it's about the lifestyle this business model creates. Flexibility is a game changer. You decide when and where you work. Maybe that's at the kitchen table while your kids are napping, or in a café with your headphones in, or even from a beach abroad if you want to combine travel with business. You're no longer bound by the rigid hours of a nine-to-five or limited by location. Your customer could be across the street or across the world, and with the click of a button you can reach them. That global reach is something brick-and-mortar businesses could only dream about a generation ago.

There's also the irresistible promise of passive income. Now, let's be clear: it's not 'passive' from day one. It takes upfront work to set up your store, research products, write descriptions, and market your brand. But once those systems are in place, your store can run while you sleep. Imagine waking up in the morning, grabbing your coffee, and checking your phone to see sales that came through overnight from customers in different time zones. That feeling, that your business is working for you even when you're not glued to a desk, is addictive.

And perhaps the biggest reason people fall in love with this path is ownership. You're not building someone else's dream. You're building yours. Every listing you create, every customer you serve, every sale you make is part of a business that belongs to you. And when it belongs to you, it becomes more than just income. It becomes a vehicle for freedom. Freedom to decide what your life looks like. Freedom to work on projects that matter to you. Freedom to take time off when you need it without asking for permission.

But it goes deeper than freedom. Online selling is also about impact. Every product you put out into the world solves a problem for someone. Maybe it's a reusable item that helps a family cut down on waste. Maybe it's a book that inspires someone to make a change in their life. Maybe it's a piece of jewellery that marks a milestone or makes someone smile. You might not always see the ripple effect, but your business touches lives. And when you do catch a glimpse through a heartfelt review or a thank-you message from a customer, you realise you're not just selling products. You're creating value.

Finally, there's legacy. For some, this starts as a side hustle. But over time, it can grow into something much bigger: a business that sustains you, employs others, or even becomes something you pass down. What begins as 'extra income 'has the potential to become an empire, built brick by brick, decision by decision. That's why so many people who start small find themselves dreaming bigger than they ever thought possible.

Now, let's get real. Online selling is powerful, but it's not magic. With all the freedom and opportunity comes responsibility and challenge. There's competition. A lot of it. If you want to stand out, you need a plan. You can't just throw up a product and hope people find it. You need to understand your audience, position your product well, and learn how to market effectively.

There are also technical challenges. You'll hear terms like SEO, PPC ads, and logistics, and at first, it might feel overwhelming. But here's the thing: every single skill you learn is an asset you keep forever. Once you figure out how to write a listing that converts or run an ad campaign that works, you can apply that skill again and again. What feels like a hurdle at first eventually becomes part of your toolkit as an entrepreneur.

Then there's risk. Not every product will be a hit. Some things you try just won't work out. But that doesn't mean you've failed. It simply means you've done market research and the market spoke. You take that information, adjust, and try again. The only true failure is quitting too soon.

Another reality is loneliness. In the beginning, you're wearing all the hats: CEO, marketer, product researcher, customer service rep. It can feel isolating, but you're not alone. There are communities of sellers, coaching programmes, and support groups where you can connect with people who get it. And once you plug into that network, the journey feels less heavy.

And above all, let's talk about self-doubt. You'll hear that little voice whispering, 'Who am I to do this? What if I fail? What if I'm not good enough?' The truth is, everyone hears that voice, even the people you look up to who seem like they have it all figured out. The difference between those who succeed and those who quit is simple: action. The only way to silence doubt is to keep moving forward.

Remember this: failure isn't final. It's feedback. Every misstep points you closer to the right path. Every challenge shapes you into a stronger entrepreneur. And every time you push past fear and take action, you're proving to yourself that you can do this.

CASE STUDIES: REAL PEOPLE, REAL SUCCESS

To make this more real, let's look at a few examples.

Caroline, the stay-at-home mum:

Caroline loved eco-friendly cleaning. She started small, selling reusable bamboo cloths on Amazon. Within two years, she built a brand earning £8,000 a month, all while being home for her kids.

Maria, the retiree:

After leaving her corporate job, Maria was lacking direction. She loved baking but couldn't open a shop. Instead, she sold baking tools and kits on Etsy and made £2,000 a month while enjoying her passion.

Daniel, the side hustler:

Daniel started designing funny T-shirts on Printful. At first, he made a few sales here and there. But when one design went viral, he earned over £20,000 in passive income in a year.

Aisha, the teacher:

Aisha wanted extra income but had no time for inventory. She turned her lesson plans into digital downloads on Etsy, selling worksheets and classroom resources. In her first year, she made £12,000 without touching a single box.

Ben, the fitness coach:

Ben published an ebook on KDP about home workouts. It didn't become a bestseller overnight, but over time it gained traction. That one book now earns him passive income every month, while also growing his personal coaching brand.

These are not superhuman people. They're ordinary people who took a chance.

WHY PEOPLE BUY ONLINE: THE PSYCHOLOGY OF ECOMMERCE

If you want to sell effectively, you need to step into the shoes of your customers and understand why they're shopping online in the first place.

At the heart of it all is convenience. People today want instant solutions. They're busy, their schedules are packed, and their patience is thinner than ever. If they can order what they need in minutes without leaving their sofa, they will. Why fight traffic, search through crowded aisles, or wait in a long queue when a product can be delivered to their doorstep with just a few taps? That's the number one reason people continue to turn to eCommerce; it saves them time, and time has become one of the most valuable currencies in modern life.

But convenience isn't the only reason. Choice plays a huge role too. Online platforms offer endless variety. A customer can compare dozens of brands, prices, styles, and reviews within seconds, something impossible in a traditional store. If they don't like one option, they can switch tabs and instantly find ten more. That sense of abundance makes online shopping irresistible.

Then there's trust. This might surprise you, because many people assume trust is harder to earn online than in person. But platforms like Amazon, Etsy, and eBay have built-in trust systems that make customers feel safe. Reviews, star ratings, buyer protection, and return policies all reduce the fear of risk. Customers don't feel like they're taking a gamble when they buy online anymore; they feel protected. And that reassurance is what keeps them coming back.

Impulse buying is another powerful driver. Think about how

often you scroll on your phone when you're bored, waiting for a bus, or lying in bed at night. That's when the majority of impulse purchases happen. Mobile shopping has turned downtime into shopping time. A catchy product video, an irresistible deal, or even just the right ad placed at the right moment can trigger a spontaneous purchase. The psychology here is simple: the easier you make it for someone to buy, the more likely they are to do it without overthinking.

And finally, there's personalisation. Thanks to algorithms and data, online shopping feels personal. Customers are shown products that seem tailor-made for them. Ads follow them around, recommendations appear like magic, and suddenly they're being offered exactly what they were just thinking about. This creates an emotional connection, a sense that the product was meant for them. It feels less like shopping and more like destiny, and that's powerful.

When you understand these drivers - convenience, choice, trust, impulse, and personalisation - you can design your listings, craft your marketing, and shape your customer experience in ways that meet people exactly where they are. You're not just selling products; you're tapping into human behaviour.

MINDSET AND MOTIVATION

Now let's shift gears. Because even when you understand the psychology of your customers, there's another psychology you need to master: your own.

Here's the truth: strategy, tools, and tactics will only get you so far. Don't get me wrong, they matter. You'll need to know how to research products, market effectively, price wisely, and navigate the practical side of online business. But what truly separates the people who succeed from the people who quit halfway isn't the perfect strategy. It's mindset.

Your business will only grow as much as you do.

And the reality is, building anything worthwhile, whether it's an online store, a brand, or even just listing your very first product, will test you. There will be moments when sales are slower than you hoped, when the tech feels overwhelming, when an ad campaign flops, or when you wonder if you're cut out for this at all. And in those moments, it won't be a tactic that saves you. It will be your mindset.

Resilience is key. You will face setbacks, that's guaranteed. A supplier might let you down, a shipment might get delayed, or a product you believed in might not sell the way you expected. But these aren't signals to quit; they're invitations to learn. Every setback carries a lesson. Resilience is about picking yourself back up, dusting yourself off, and trying again with a little more wisdom than before. It's like a muscle: the more you use it, the stronger it gets.

Then comes patience. In today's world, where we're used to instant everything - food delivered in minutes, films streamed instantly, information at our fingertips - patience feels old fashioned. But when it comes to business, patience is everything. Success doesn't happen overnight. It's built sale by sale, lesson by lesson, brick by brick. Some people give up too soon because they expect instant results. The winners are the ones who keep going, even when progress feels slow.

And let's talk about confidence. Here's the big secret: you don't need to have it all figured out before you begin. You don't need to know everything about eCommerce, marketing, or branding to take your first step. Confidence doesn't magically appear before you start. It grows as you take action. The more you do, the more confident you become. The first step might feel messy, awkward, or uncertain, but it's the step that matters most.

Remember this: every expert you admire was once a beginner. Every thriving brand you see today - whether it's a household name or a small online shop with a loyal following - started with a single product, a single listing, a single sale. No one wakes up successful. They build it, piece by piece, often failing forward along the way.

That's why your job is not to be perfect. Your job is simply to begin. Because once you begin, you set momentum in motion. And momentum is what turns a dream into a business.

EXERCISE: PRACTICAL MINDSET TOOLS

So, how do you actually strengthen your mindset? Here are a few tools you can start using today:

- ***Morning Affirmations.***

Start your day with intention. Instead of rolling over and scrolling Instagram, say something powerful to yourself:

'I am building a business that gives me freedom and impact. Every step I take is moving me closer to the life I want.'

It might feel silly at first, but your brain believes what you tell it consistently.

- ***Journaling.***

At the end of each week, take ten minutes to reflect. Ask yourself:

What worked this week?

What didn't?

What did I learn?

This habit keeps you focused on progress instead of perfection.

- ***Micro-Wins.***

Don't wait until you've hit £10,000 in sales to celebrate. Celebrate the first product you list, the first review you receive, the first £10 in profit. These 'small' wins are actually huge. They build momentum, and momentum builds confidence.

- ***Reframing Failure.***

When something doesn't go the way you planned, don't label it as failure. Call it feedback.

Say: 'This didn't work. What can I try differently next time?'

That shift alone will keep you moving forward when others give up.

Here's what I want you to hold onto: your job is not to be perfect. Your job is to begin.

If you show up with resilience, patience, and confidence, even in small doses, you'll already be ahead of most people who quit before they see what's possible.

ACTIVITY

Grab a notebook or open a document. Let's make this personal.

Step 1: Define Your Why

Why do you want to sell online? Write your true reason: freedom, income, flexibility, impact.

Step 2: Visualise Your Dream Life

Imagine it's one year from today. Your store is live. Sales are coming in.

How much are you earning?

Where are you working?

How do you feel when you wake up?

Step 3: Name Your Fears

List your top three fears about starting.

Then write one way you could handle each fear.

Example: Fear of failure > Commit to testing small before scaling.

Step 4: Discover Your Strengths

Write down three strengths you already have.

(Are you organised? Creative? Good with people? Tech-curious?)

Step 5: Plan Your First Step

Decide on one simple action to take this week.

Research platforms.

Brainstorm product ideas.

Join a seller Facebook group.

Step 6: Commit

Sign your name under this statement:

'I commit to taking the first step in building my online business this week. My future self deserves it.'

Keep this exercise close. It's your compass. On tough days, it will remind you why you started.

This is your starting line. Your fresh page.

Forget the idea that you have to be an expert to begin. You don't. You just have to start.

So, what will you build? Who will you reach? What impact will your products have in someone else's life?

That's what we're here to discover.

Let's move on to Chapter 2, where we'll start mapping out your platform and niche, the foundation of your future business.

Your journey begins now.

CHAPTER 2:

CHOOSING YOUR PATH

You've learned what's possible. You've glimpsed the world of online selling and what it can unlock for everyday people. Now it's time to get focused. In this chapter, we're going to take everything you've absorbed so far and begin laying the real foundation of your future online eCommerce business.

We'll skip the comparison of marketplaces; that's already behind us. You know platforms like Etsy, eBay, Shopify, and TikTok Shop exist. You understand that each has strengths and quirks. But for the remainder of this book, we're zeroing in on one platform: Amazon.

Why Amazon? Because it offers the fastest route to traction. It's where the buyers are — hundreds of millions of them. It's not just a marketplace; it's a search engine for products. It comes with trust, infrastructure, and built-in demand. If you're serious about turning an idea into income, Amazon is one of the most powerful tools you can leverage.

But before we dive into tools, tactics, and product strategies, we need to address the elephant in the room.

Shifting from 'Hobby Thinking' to 'Business Thinking'

This shift in mindset is non-negotiable. If you treat this like a hobby - a casual experiment with no accountability or long-term vision - that's exactly how it will pay you: casually. If, however, you commit to treating it like a business from day one, the entire landscape changes.

Here's what that shift looks like:

Hobby Thinking:

- ***'Let me see if this works.'***
- ***"I'll try when I have time.'***
- ***"I hope people buy it.'***
- ***"I'm not good at marketing.'***
- ***"It's just a side project.'***

Business Thinking:

- ***"Let's figure out what the market needs.'***
- ***"I will schedule time like it's my job.'***
- ***"I will test, refine, and relaunch until it sells.'***
- ***"Marketing is a skill and I can learn it.'***
- ***"This is a business, and I am its founder.'***

This single shift will change everything. It will drive your decisions. It will keep you going when results are slow. And it will prepare you to make smart, strategic choices - starting with your business model.

BUSINESS MODELS ON AMAZON EXPLAINED

Amazon isn't just one model. It's an ecosystem. There are multiple ways to build a business on Amazon, each with its own pros, cons, and learning curve. Here's a breakdown of the most common models:

1. Fulfilled by Amazon (FBA)

With FBA, you send your products to Amazon's warehouses. Amazon stores your inventory, handles packing, shipping, returns, and customer service.

Pros:

Prime badge (faster shipping, higher trust)

Amazon handles logistics

Great for growing and scaling

Cons:

Storage and fulfilment fees

Less control over inventory

Best for: People who want a hands-off fulfilment process and to grow globally, quickly.

2. Fulfilled by Merchant (FBM)

With FBM, you list products on Amazon but ship them yourself (or through a third-party provider).

Pros:

More control over packaging and inventory

Potentially higher margins

Cons:

You handle fulfilment, returns, and customer service

Best for: Sellers with handmade items, fragile goods, or those wanting to test without upfront inventory commitments.

3. Retail Arbitrage (RA)

You buy discounted or clearance items in physical stores and resell them on Amazon for a profit.

Pros:

Low start-up cost

Immediate opportunity

Cons:

Time intensive

Inconsistent inventory

Amazon may restrict some brands

Best for: Beginners learning the ropes without major financial risk.

4. Online Arbitrage (OA)

Same concept as RA, but you source products online rather than in-store.

Pros:

Can be done from anywhere

Scalable with tools

Cons:

More competition

Smaller profit margins

Best for: Those comfortable with online research and automation tools.

5. Wholesale

You buy bulk products from brands or distributors at wholesale prices and resell them on Amazon.

Pros:

Predictable inventory

Easier to scale than arbitrage

Cons:

Requires upfront capital

Relationship building required

Best for: Sellers ready to build relationships with suppliers and scale professionally.

6. Private Label

You create your own branded version of an existing product. This is the most scalable and brandable model.

Pros:

Brand ownership

Higher profit potential

Easier to build long-term value

Cons:

Higher upfront investment

Learning curve around sourcing, branding, and marketing

Best for: Sellers serious about long-term growth, willing to invest time and money.

HOW TO CHOOSE THE RIGHT MODEL FOR YOU

Ask yourself:

How much time and capital can I invest?

Do I want to build a brand or make quick flips?

Do I enjoy research and sourcing?

Am I ready to commit for the long haul?

If you're starting with low capital and want to learn he ropes:

Start with RA, OA, or FBM.

If you're ready to invest and build a brand:

Consider FBA with Private Label or Wholesale.

Now that you understand your model options, it's time to talk about the engine of every Amazon business.

THE POWER OF NICHE: WHY SPECIFICITY WINS

Choosing a niche is one of the most important decisions you'll make. It determines your audience, your messaging, your product direction, and your marketing strategy.

A niche isn't just a product category. It's a community of people with shared problems, desires, and language. The more you understand them, the easier it is to sell.

Why Niche Down?

- ***Easier to stand out***
- ***Easier to build trust***
- ***Easier to become an authority***
- ***Easier to scale with complementary products***

Examples:

'Fitness' is not a niche. It's a category.

'Fitness for busy mums over 40' is a niche.

'Home decor' is not a niche.

'Boho-inspired, eco-friendly home decor for small apartments' is a niche.

Don't be afraid to get specific. Specific sells.

TOOLS FOR NICHE DISCOVERY

Here are some ways to identify a profitable niche:

1. Amazon Best Sellers

Browse by category. Look for patterns. What keeps showing up? Are there sub-niches with high demand but less saturation?

2. Helium 10 / Jungle Scout

These tools help analyse sales data, competition, and keywords. You can validate niche demand before you invest.

3. Facebook Groups

Find communities with passionate, active members. What are they buying? Complaining about? Wishing existed?

4. Google Trends

Check if your niche is growing or declining. Seasonal? Evergreen?

5. Your Own Life

What do you buy? What problems have you solved? What do your friends ask you for advice about?

EXERCISE & ACTIVITY

NICHE CLARITY MAP

Take out a notebook or open a document and answer:

What hobbies, jobs, or life experiences do I have?

What products do I use daily that others might not know about?

What communities do I belong to?

What brands or products do I wish existed?

What problems do I hear people in my circle talking about?

Use your answers to brainstorm niche ideas. Then validate them using Amazon or a research tool.

AVOID THESE BEGINNER NICHE MISTAKES

Chasing trends blindly.

Fidget spinners were hot... until they weren't. Look for consistent demand.

Picking a niche you hate.

If you're not interested in the topic, you'll burn out.

Going too broad.

'Pet supplies 'is too general.

Try: 'Dog grooming for small dog breeds.'

Ignoring competition.

Competition means demand, but don't pick a saturated niche with no clear angle.

Skipping research.

Gut instinct is great, but data should lead your decision.

FINAL THOUGHTS

Build with intention.

By now, you should be thinking more like a business owner. You've:

- ***Chosen Amazon as your platform***
- ***Learned about multiple business models***

- ***Started considering which model fits your strengths***
- ***Begun exploring niche ideas and tools***

This is the groundwork. The blueprint. The beginning of your strategy.

In the next chapter, we'll dive into getting started as an Amazon seller and how to find winning products that align with your niche, your goals, and your chosen model.

You're no longer just thinking. You're building.

Let's keep going!

PART 2: MASTERING AMAZON BASICS

CHAPTER 3:

SETTING UP SHOP THE RIGHT WAY

Welcome to the foundational chapter that bridges intention and action. By now, you've clarified your motivation, chosen Amazon as your platform, explored business models, and mapped out your niche. Now, it's time to roll up your sleeves and dive into the logistics of actually becoming a seller. This chapter is about getting set up the right way, smartly, legally and strategically, so you can scale with confidence.

Before we delve into the exciting world of becoming an Amazon seller, let us take a quick trip down memory lane. Amazon, the undisputed king of eCommerce, boasts a fascinating history that reflects the company's commitment to innovation and customer obsession.

In 1994, Jeff Bezos, a visionary entrepreneur with a passion for books, started Amazon as a humble online bookstore operating out of his garage. Back then, the internet was in its nascent stages, and the idea of buying books online seemed like a futuristic concept. However, Bezos believed in the power of the internet to revolutionise the way we shop.

Amazon's initial focus on a vast selection of books at competitive prices, coupled with its innovative one-click ordering system, quickly propelled it to success. The company did not stop there. Throughout the years, Amazon has continuously expanded its product offerings, venturing into music, electronics, home goods and virtually anything you can imagine.

A Pioneering Spirit

Here are some milestones that solidified Amazon's position as a game-changer in the eCommerce landscape:

1997:

Amazon becomes a publicly traded company, signalling the confidence investors had in its disruptive potential.

1998:

The launch of Amazon Prime membership offered expedited shipping and other perks, creating a loyal customer base.

2006:

Amazon Web Services (AWS) is born, revolutionising cloud computing and generating a significant revenue stream for the company.

2014:

The introduction of the Amazon Echo ushers in the era of smart speakers and voice-controlled shopping.

Today, Amazon stands as a global eCommerce giant, renowned for its vast selection, efficient fulfilment systems and commitment to customer satisfaction. As you embark on your journey to become an Amazon seller, you are tapping into a rich legacy of innovation and a platform that empowers countless entrepreneurs to achieve their eCommerce dreams.

Now that you are armed with a brief historical perspective, let us get you started on setting up your very own Amazon Seller account. In the next step, I will guide you through the registration process and ensure you are ready to conquer the Amazon marketplace.

But before you unleash your inner entrepreneur on the Amazon platform, there are some key steps to navigate. In this chapter, I will guide you through the process of becoming a successful Amazon seller, from setting up your account to mastering the art of product listing and fulfilment. So buckle up and get ready to conquer the Amazon colossus.

In this chapter, we will embark on a journey to set up your Seller Central account, which will serve as your mission control centre for all your Amazon selling activities. From listing products and managing inventory to tracking sales and interacting with customers, Seller Central will be your one-stop shop for managing your Amazon business. By the end of this chapter, you will be equipped to navigate the registration process and unlock the full potential of your Seller Central account.

Choosing Your Selling Plan

There are two main selling plans on Amazon: Individual and Professional. Deciding which one is right for you depends on your business volume and goals. Here is a quick breakdown.

Individual Selling Plans

Individual selling on Amazon is not just a transaction; it is the start of a journey. As a solo entrepreneur, you have the freedom to curate your products, tell your story and build a brand that resonates with your vision. Perfect for beginners with a limited number of products (selling fewer than forty items per month). Embrace the power of one - your unique voice in a global marketplace.

Here are key details:

- ***Ideal for occasional and low-volume sellers.***
- ***No monthly fees, but there is a £0.75 (or $0.99) fee per item sold.***
- ***Limited to selling up to forty units each month.***
- ***Perfect if you are testing your products or selling a few items here and there.***

Professional Selling Plans

Ideal for established businesses or those with a higher sales volume. A Professional Selling Plan on Amazon is designed for sellers who anticipate selling more than forty items per month. Aspiring entrepreneurs and established brands alike can harness the power of professional selling on Amazon to unlock new horizons and elevate their business to unprecedented heights.

Here are the key details:

- ***IMonthly Subscription Fee: £25 + VAT or $39.99 per month, regardless of how many items you sell.***
- ***INo Per-Item Sold Fee: Professional sellers do not pay a fee for each item sold.***

Additional Features:

- ***Bulk listing: easily list multiple products at once.***
- ***Advertising: access advertising tools to promote your products.***
- ***Top placement: eligibility for top placement on product detail pages.***

Whether you are a seasoned seller or just starting out, the Professional Selling Plan provides the tools you need to grow your business on Amazon.

ACCOUNT TYPES EXPLAINED

Individual Seller Account

For inexperienced sellers or those with a small selection of products, an Individual Seller Account serves as a basic entry point into the world of online sales. Sellers can use this platform without paying a monthly subscription charge and can list products in more than twenty categories.

Although its low cost and simplicity may be appealing, the Individual Seller Account has limitations. Selling fees per item and the inability to compete in restricted categories may limit growth and cost-effectiveness for sellers with larger sales volumes. Therefore, sellers with fewer products and lower volumes are best suited for this account type.

There is no monthly membership cost; however, individual accounts incur a £0.75 or $0.99 fee for each item sold. This fee structure works well for small-scale sellers but can become expensive for those managing higher quantities.

Professional Seller Account

Amazon's premium option designed to satisfy the intricate needs of agencies and high-volume sellers is the Professional Seller Account. All product categories are accessible without limitations and advanced selling tools are included in this comprehensive plan.

Strong features include bulk listing and reporting tools, spreadsheet and API-based inventory management, shipping rate customisation and Sponsored Products. These features promote an environment suited to efficiency and scalability.

Key advantages include:

- ***Comprehensive inventory and order management***
- ***Expanded category access***
- ***No per-item selling fees***

Although the Professional Seller Account carries a £25 or $39.99 monthly subscription charge, the absence of per-item fees compensates for this at higher sales volumes. Sellers should note that referral fees and closing fees may still apply depending on the category.

For companies aiming for significant growth and high sales volumes, the Professional Seller Account is cost-effective and scalable.

Amazon Seller Central

Through the web-based infrastructure known as Amazon Seller Central, both professional and individual seller accounts can offer their goods directly on Amazon's marketplace. Sellers can manage their inventory, product listings, pricing and order fulfilment from this central location.

You can use Seller Central to:

- ***Track your sales results***
- ***Obtain customer feedback***
- ***Add new listings or update existing ones***
- ***Produce business reports***
- ***Monitor refunds, returns and payments***

Amazon Vendor Central Account

The Amazon Vendor Central account is another essential component of the Amazon ecosystem. It serves as an alternative to the Professional Seller account and is designed for suppliers or manufacturers who want to sell directly to Amazon.

How to Get a Vendor Central Account

Vendor Central membership is by invitation only. Amazon will reach out when it sees potential for a mutually beneficial wholesale relationship.

If Amazon is interested in buying your products in bulk, they will invite you to apply. With this approach, Amazon purchases goods from suppliers and assumes responsibility for selling them to customers. This eliminates many administrative responsibilities associated with fulfilment, returns and customer support.

However, Vendor Central has disadvantages. Sellers may have less control over product listings, and pricing negotiations with Amazon can be challenging. While Amazon manages many of the intricate aspects of selling, you must still negotiate effectively to maintain profitability.

DECIDING BETWEEN AMAZON SELLER CENTRAL AND VENDOR CENTRAL

Let us break down the differences to help you decide.

Aspect	Seller Central	Vendor Central
Inventory Management	Manage your inventory.	Amazon buys in bulk and manages your inventory.
Pricing	Set and adjust your product prices.	Amazon controls pricing, buying wholesale and selling to customers.
Marketing Tools	Use tools like Sponsored Products	Access additional tools like Amazon Vine and A+ content.
Decision Factors	Consider business model, size, and control.	Weigh pros and cons for long-term business goals.

Selecting between Seller Central and Vendor Central requires thoughtful consideration. Evaluate your business model, company size and preferred level of control. Each platform has pros and cons and the choice should align with your long-term goals.

From my experience over the last decade, fewer brands choose Vendor Central due to the impact on profitability and flexibility.

DOCUMENTS REQUIRED TO SELL ON AMAZON

Your adventure through the world of eCommerce starts the moment you click the sign up as a seller button on Amazon. There is still a lot to come because this is just the beginning.

It's not too difficult to register for an Amazon seller account, but to make the process go more smoothly, we always advise beginners to develop a list of the items they will need before registering. We will provide you with all the information and documentation required for you to begin selling on Amazon immediately.

The Following are the documents and information needed to embark on your Amazon seller career and start selling on the platform.

Business Data

Your address, phone number, and business name will be included in this. Verify that all of the information is current and accurate. To ensure that you have no issues when authenticating your seller account, you must supply your most recent contact details.

Individual information

It should go without saying that you will do this when you create the account. To register for an Amazon account, provide your name, phone number, and functional email address. To ensure that you receive all critical emails straight into your email account without any issues, use your personal email address. Government ID Passport or driver's license of the primary account holder and it must match the name on the account

Bank Card

A legitimate credit card number and billing address are required. Your account will be closed if your credit card is invalid or if Amazon is unable to validate it. As a result, you must ensure that all of your credit card information is correct.

Telephone Number

For verification purposes, you must have a functional phone number where others may reach you with ease. When registering, make sure you have your phone handy since Amazon will call or text you to confirm your identification.

Tax Identification

In addition to your Social Security number. National Insurance number you must provide your tax identification number. If you are a business, you must enter the Company Registration details.

EXERCISE AND ACTIVITY

Ready to take the plunge? Here is a step-by-step guide to creating your Seller Central account:

- ***Visit https://sellercentral.amazon.com/ or sell.amazon.co.uk and click on 'Create your Amazon Seller Account.'***
- ***Choose your selling plan (Individual or Professional).***
- ***Enter your business and contact information.***
- ***Provide your tax identification number and bank account details.***
- ***Review Amazon's terms and conditions and agree.***

Congratulations. You have successfully created your Seller Central account.

Completion Check

Have you navigated the registration process and are you ready to create your Seller Central account? (Yes or No)

By answering 'Yes' to the Completion Check, you are ready to delve deeper into the world of Amazon product research and selection in the next chapter. If you encounter any difficulties during registration, feel free to ask and we can explore helpful resources together.

Once approved, you will gain access to Seller Central and can begin listing your first products.

SETTING YOURSELF UP FOR LONG-TERM SUCCESS

Creating a seller account is just the first step. Let us discuss how to build a foundation that supports consistent growth.

1. Treat It Like a Real Business

This is not just about selling things online. This is about building a brand.

That means:

- ***Separating your personal and business finances***
- ***Keeping accurate records for tax and inventory***
- ***Setting goals for revenue and reinvestment***
- ***Maintaining professional communication with customers***

2. Choose the Right Business Model

Revisiting the models briefly:

FBA (Fulfilment by Amazon)

- ***Amazon handles warehousing, packing, shipping and customer service***
- ***You focus on product sourcing and marketing***
- ***Best for scalability and passive income potential***

FBM (Fulfilled by Merchant)

- ***You ship products directly to customers***
- ***Lower fees and more control***
- ***Best for handmade items, custom goods or local sellers***

Retail Arbitrage

- ***Buy discounted items in retail stores and resell on Amazon***
- ***Quick cash flow but time intensive***
- ***Best for beginners wanting to learn the ropes***

Online Arbitrage

- ***Buy discounted items online and resell at a profit***
- ***Can be scaled with virtual assistants and software***

Wholesale

- ***Buy in bulk directly from brands or distributors***
- ***Lower margins but higher volume***
- ***More stable and scalable than arbitrage***

Private Label

- ***Create your own brand of an existing product***

- ***Higher start-up costs but long-term control***
- ***Ideal for building a sellable asset***

3. Create Systems Early

Do not wait until things get chaotic. Set up:

- ***A digital filing system (Google Drive, Dropbox, Notion)***
- ***Bookkeeping software (QuickBooks, Xero, Wave)***
- ***Inventory tracking tools (InventoryLab, Helium 10, Sellerboard)***
- ***Email templates for customer service***

4. Understand Amazon's Rules

Amazon is strict. Sellers who do not follow the rules risk suspension. Familiarise yourself with:

- ***Prohibited products***
- ***Listing guidelines***
- ***Review policies***
- ***Seller metrics (late shipment rate, order defect rate, cancellation rate)***

Stay in good standing and Amazon will reward you with more visibility and fewer issues.

5. Think Long Term: Branding, Not Just Selling

Even if you start with arbitrage or wholesale, think about the bigger picture. Ask yourself:

- ***Can I grow a customer base?***
- ***Could I expand into complementary products?***
- ***How can I create packaging that reflects my identity?***
- ***Would this business be attractive to a buyer one day?***

6. Surround Yourself with Support

This journey is easier when you are not alone. Consider:

- ***Joining Amazon seller communities (Facebook groups, Reddit, Discord)***
- ***Subscribing to newsletters and podcasts***
- ***Investing in courses or coaching***

The more knowledge you absorb, the faster you will avoid pitfalls and seize opportunities.

ACTIVITY

Take time now to:

- ***Gather your registration documents***
- ***Choose your seller plan***
- ***Set up your Seller Central account***
- ***Decide which business model fits your current lifestyle and goals***

In the next chapter, we will explore finding winning products, arguably the most exciting and critical step in your Amazon journey. Even the best setup cannot succeed without products that people truly want to buy.

You have laid the foundation. Now let us build something incredible.

PART 2: MASTERING AMAZON BASICS

CHAPTER 4:

PRODUCT RESEARCH MADE SIMPLE

Congratulations on setting up your Seller Central account! Now comes the exciting part: finding the perfect products to sell on Amazon.

Imagine this. You have invested time and effort in listing a product on Amazon, only to see crickets chirping, figuratively speaking, when it comes to sales. Ouch. The key to avoiding this scenario lies in product research. This crucial step involves identifying profitable products with high demand and low competition, ensuring your listings attract a steady stream of customers.

In this chapter, you will become a master product researcher, wielding powerful tools and strategies to discover the hidden gems that will propel your Amazon business to success. So grab your creative spark and let's delve into the world of Amazon product research.

Identifying Profitable Products to Sell on Amazon

Properly conducting product research on Amazon is essential

for success on the platform. Selecting the right products to offer becomes easier when you evaluate pricing, competition, customer feedback and sales history. However, navigating Amazon without guidance can be intimidating due to the marketplace's vast size and pace.

What Does Product Research on Amazon Do?

Amazon product research involves analysing competing items, consumer preferences and market trends to find lucrative opportunities. It helps sellers identify the best products to market and sell. In such a competitive space, product research aims to optimise sales, customer satisfaction and overall performance.

Four Steps to Amazon Product Research

Although navigating this enormous marketplace can feel overwhelming, there are clear steps you can follow to streamline your research. Here is a step-by-step guide to help you determine profitable products, understand consumer demand and outperform competitors.

Determine Which Market to Target

Prioritise identifying your target market, tracking new trends and understanding customer preferences. This approach helps you choose products that meet the needs of your audience.

Outline the Demographics of Your Customers

To conduct effective product research, you must know your target market. Begin by establishing your audience's demographics, such as location, income, gender and age. The more you understand about them, the better you can tailor your product choices.

Examine Current and Upcoming Trends

Analyse emerging trends on Amazon to stay ahead of the competition. Use resources such as Google Trends and other eCommerce platforms to discover popular products. By monitoring best sellers, top sales and trending items, you can identify opportunities that match your target audience's preferences.

Look Up Customer Feedback, Reviews and Preferences

Investigate consumer preferences, testimonials and comments to gain insight into your market. By reading customer reviews, you can identify both strengths and weaknesses in existing products.

Look for patterns such as:

- ***Consumer complaints***
- ***Recurring purchase trends***
- ***Price points and pricing strategies***
- ***Shipping expectations***
- ***Overall user experience***

This information will improve your research and boost your chances of selecting a successful product.

Amazon Tools to Research Products

The right tools make product research faster and more accurate. These resources offer features such as:

- ***Past sales information***
- ***Keyword research***
- ***Competitor analysis***

- ***Data accuracy***
- ***Sales estimates***
- ***Potential profit insights***
- ***Shipping cost evaluations***
- ***Sales performance forecasts***

Combine free tools like Google Trends with the popular Amazon-focused tools below.

Google Trends

Google Trends provides free data on the popularity of search terms over time. It allows you to compare interest in specific keywords and identify long-term patterns.

This tool helps you understand search volume and niche popularity. Tracking search themes related to your product can highlight whether interest is rising, falling or seasonal, enabling you to make better choices about what to stock.

Alongside Google Trends, you can strengthen your research using Jungle Scout, AMZScout and Helium 10, which offer more Amazon-specific insights.

Jungle Scout is my favourite tool and I call it my Amazon spyware! It helps Amazon sellers investigate competitors, evaluate product trends, forecast sales figures and identify lucrative opportunities in the marketplace.

AMZScout is a popular tool that offers competitor analysis, sales predictions and product research features to help sellers make informed business decisions.

Helium 10 is a comprehensive toolkit built for Amazon sellers. It provides product research, competitor analysis, listing optimisation, inventory management and keyword research tools.

Analysing Market Demand, Competition and Profit Margins

Analysing Market Demand

Evaluating market demand helps you identify products likely to succeed.

Here is a simple guide to analysing demand:

1. Keyword Research

Identify relevant keywords for your product. Use Amazon's search bar suggestions, Google Keyword Planner or tools like Jungle Scout, MerchantWords or Helium 10. Search behaviour gives insight into customer interest.

2. Check Best Sellers and Top-Rated Products

Explore Amazon's Best Sellers and Top-Rated sections. They reveal trending products and common customer preferences. Pay attention to reviews, as they reveal pain points and desires.

Analysing Competitors

Analysing your competitors uncovers opportunities and reveals gaps in the market.

Finding the Best Performers

Competitor analysis is essential. Focus on products with strong Best Sellers Rank (BSR) and consistent search visibility. Products with high positive review counts indicate satisfied demand.

Browse 'Frequently Bought Together' and 'Customers Also Bought' sections to identify cross-selling opportunities and related niches.

Finding top performers gives you clear insight into what sells and why.

Analysing Profit Margins

Analysing profit margins on Amazon is crucial for effective product research and making informed decisions about which products to sell. Here's a step-by-step guide on how to analyse profit margins:

1. Determine Selling Price:

- ***Identify potential products you're interested in selling.***
- ***Research the current selling prices of similar products on Amazon.***
- ***Consider your pricing strategy and determine the price at which you plan to sell your product.***

2. Calculate Amazon Fees:

Understand the various fees associated with selling on Amazon, including referral fees, fulfillment fees (if using Fulfillment by Amazon - FBA), and subscription fees (if applicable).

Use the Amazon Fee Calculator or refer to Amazon's Fee Schedule to estimate these fees for your specific product category and pricing.

3. Factor in Shipping Costs:

Include the cost of shipping the product to Amazon's fulfillment centre if you're using FBA.

Consider any inbound shipping costs, customs fees, or other logistical expenses.

Estimate Cost of Goods Sold (COGS):

Calculate the cost of manufacturing or purchasing your product.

Include any additional costs such as packaging, labelling, and quality control.

Calculate Gross Profit:

Subtract the total costs (Amazon fees, shipping, and COGS) from the selling price to determine your gross profit.

Determine Gross Profit Margin:

To calculate the gross profit margin, divide it by the selling price and multiply by 100 to get the percentage.

Consider Additional Costs:

To calculate the gross profit margin, divide it by the selling price and multiply by 100 to get the percentage.

Evaluate Competitor Pricing:

Analyse the pricing strategies of competitors selling similar products.

Consider whether you can offer a competitive price while maintaining a satisfactory profit margin.

Monitor Market Trends:

Stay informed about market trends and demand fluctuations that might impact pricing and profitability.

Be flexible in adjusting your pricing strategy based on market dynamics.

Use Profit Analytics Tools:

Leverage Amazon's Seller Central tools and third-party analytics tools to track and analyse your sales and profitability.

Regularly review and update your profit margin calculations to ensure they align with your business goals.

By systematically analysing profit margins and considering all associated costs, you can make informed decisions about the viability of selling a particular product on Amazon. Remember that maintaining a healthy profit margin is essential for the long-term success of your e-commerce business.

SOURCING STRATEGIES: WHERE DO YOU FIND YOUR PRODUCTS?

Once you've identified your desired product, it's time to source it! Here are some common options:

Manufacturers:

One of the primary sourcing options for Amazon sellers is establishing direct relationships with manufacturers. This involves working closely with a company that produces the goods you intend to sell. This option is ideal for entrepreneurs looking to create a unique, branded product. While the initial investment and commitment may be higher, it provides greater control over product quality, customisation, and pricing. Source directly from the manufacturer if you require high customisation or large quantities.

Advantages:

Quality Control: Sourcing directly from the manufacturer gives you the greatest control over product quality. You can specify materials, production processes, and quality control measures to ensure your product meets your exact standards.

Potentially Lower Costs: By eliminating intermediaries like wholesalers, you might negotiate more competitive pricing, especially for high-volume orders. This allows you to offer attractive prices to customers while maintaining healthy profit margins.

Customisation Options: Many manufacturers offer customisation possibilities, such as private labelling or custom packaging. This allows you to create a unique brand identity and differentiate yourself from competitors.

Disadvantages:

Higher Minimum Order Quantities (MOQs): Manufacturers often have minimum order quantities (MOQs) that can be significant, especially for overseas manufacturers. This can require a substantial upfront investment in inventory, which might not be ideal for new sellers.

Communication Challenges: If sourcing from overseas manufacturers, communication barriers can arise due to language or time zone differences. Building clear communication protocols and establishing a reliable relationship with your supplier is essential.

Lead Times: Manufacturing products, especially with customisations, takes time. Factor in lead times for production and shipping when planning your inventory levels to avoid stockouts.

Example: Let's say you've identified a niche for ergonomic laptop stands. Through your research, you discover a manufacturer in China that produces high-quality stands with customisable features like adjustable angles and built-in phone holders. By working directly with the manufacturer, you can ensure the quality meets your standards, potentially negotiate a competitive price for bulk orders, and explore customisation options to create a unique brand identity for your ergonomic laptop stands.

However, you'll need to consider the minimum order quantity (MOQ) set by the manufacturer. If the MOQ is 1000 units, you'll need to be confident you can sell that amount of inventory to recoup your investment. Additionally, communication with the manufacturer might involve time zone differences and potential language barriers. Building a strong working relationship and clear communication protocols will be crucial.

Remember: Sourcing directly from manufacturers can be a rewarding strategy, especially for established sellers with the capital to handle higher minimum order quantities.

Wholesalers:

Wholesalers act as intermediaries between manufacturers and retailers, offering bulk quantities of products at discounted rates. This option is beneficial for Amazon sellers who want to carry a diverse range of products without managing the complexities of manufacturing. Wholesalers provide scalability and convenience, allowing entrepreneurs to focus on marketing and sales. However, be mindful of competition, as wholesalers may supply the same products to multiple sellers.

Advantages:

Lower Minimum Order Quantities: Wholesalers typically offer lower minimum order quantities compared to manufacturers. This allows you to test different products and keep your initial investment lower, which is ideal for new sellers or those with limited capital.

Variety and Scalability: Wholesalers often carry a vast selection of products across various categories. This allows you to curate a diverse product range for your Amazon store without the complexities of managing multiple manufacturing relationships. As your business grows, you can easily scale your inventory by increasing your orders with the wholesaler.

Convenience: Wholesalers handle product sourcing, storage, and sometimes even shipping logistics. This frees you up to focus on essential tasks like marketing your products and managing your Amazon store, saving you valuable time and resources.

Disadvantages:

Lower Profit Margins: Since wholesalers buy products in bulk from manufacturers and then sell them to retailers like you, the profit margin per item might be lower compared to sourcing directly from a manufacturer.

Competition: Many wholesalers supply the same products to multiple sellers on Amazon. This can increase competition and make it challenging to stand out unless you have a strong brand identity or unique marketing strategies.

Limited Control Over Quality: While reputable wholesalers typically maintain quality standards, you might have less control over the manufacturing process compared to sourcing directly from a manufacturer. It's crucial to choose a reliable wholesaler with a proven track record of quality products.

Example: Imagine you've identified a niche for trendy phone cases. Through your research, you discover a wholesaler that offers a wide variety of phone cases for different phone models, featuring popular designs and materials like silicone or vegan leather. Sourcing from a wholesaler allows you to offer a diverse selection of phone cases without the need to manage individual manufacturing relationships. The lower minimum order quantities enable you to test different styles and designs without a significant upfront investment.

However, you'll need to be mindful of potential competition. Since the wholesaler supplies phone cases to other sellers, you might face competition on price and product offerings. To differentiate yourself, consider creating a strong brand identity for your store, focusing on excellent customer service, or offering unique bundles or gift sets with your phone cases.

Wholesalers offer a convenient and scalable solution for Amazon sellers, especially those starting or looking to manage a diverse product range.

Print on Demand (POD):

For entrepreneurs with a creative flair or niche market focus, print on demand (POD) is an attractive option. POD allows you to customise and print your designs on various products, such as apparel, accessories, and home goods, without holding inventory. This minimises upfront costs and storage concerns, making it a low-risk option for testing new ideas and targeting specific audiences. Keep in mind that profit margins may be lower compared to other sourcing methods. This option allows you to sell custom-designed products without holding inventory (great for t-shirts, mugs, etc.).

Advantages:

Low Upfront Costs & No Inventory Management: POD is a dream come true for creative entrepreneurs and those with limited startup capital. You don't need to invest in bulk inventory or manage storage space. Simply upload your designs, and the POD provider handles printing your designs on various products upon receiving customer orders. This eliminates the risk of overstocking or deadstock (inventory that doesn't sell).

Testing & Customisation: POD allows you to experiment with different product designs and target specific niches without a significant financial commitment. You can create unique t-shirts, mugs, phone cases, or even home décor items featuring your designs or slogans. This is a fantastic way to test the market and gauge customer interest before scaling up your product offerings.

On-Demand Fulfilllment: Since POD printing happens upon receiving an order, you never have to worry about fulfilling orders yourself or managing stock levels. The POD provider takes care of production and shipping, freeing you up to focus on marketing and customer service.

Disadvantages:

Lower Profit Margins: POD providers charge per-item printing fees, which can eat into your profit margins compared to other sourcing methods like bulk wholesale buying. Carefully analyse the POD provider's pricing structure and factor in these costs when determining your product pricing strategy.

Limited Control over Quality: While reputable POD providers maintain high-quality standards, you might have less control over the printing process and product materials compared to working directly with a manufacturer. It's crucial to choose a POD provider known for excellent print quality and durability.

Design Limitations: Some POD providers may have limitations on the type of designs you can upload or the available product options. Familiarise yourself with the POD provider's design guidelines and product offerings before finalising your product concept.

Example: Let's say you're an artist with a passion for creating quirky animal illustrations. You see potential in the pet accessories niche and decide to explore POD. A popular POD provider allows you to upload your illustrations and customise various pet products, from bandanas and collars to tote bags and water bowls. This allows you to showcase your artwork on a variety of products without the risk of holding excess inventory.

However, you'll need to consider the profit margins. Since the POD provider charges per-item printing fees, your profit margin per bandana or tote bag might be lower compared to bulk ordering from a manufacturer. To counteract this, you can explore premium product options offered by the POD provider, such as organic cotton or double-sided printing, and adjust your pricing accordingly.

POD is a fantastic option for creative entrepreneurs, those with niche product ideas, or anyone hesitant about large upfront inventory investments.

Dropshipping:

Dropshipping is a popular and increasingly prevalent method for Amazon sellers. With dropshipping, you partner with suppliers who handle inventory, packing, and shipping directly to customers. This model minimises the need for large upfront investments in inventory, storage, and fulfillment infrastructure. While it offers flexibility and a lower financial barrier to entry, sellers should be cautious about potential challenges, such as longer shipping times and less control over the fulfillment process.

Advantages:

Low Startup Costs: The biggest perk of dropshipping is the minimal financial commitment needed to get started. You don't have to invest in bulk inventory or manage storage space. This allows you to test the waters with various products without a significant financial risk.

Scalability and Flexibility: Dropshipping offers excellent scalability. As your sales grow, you can easily expand your product offerings without worrying about managing additional inventory. It also provides flexibility – you can add or remove products from your store quickly based on market trends or customer demand.

Convenience and Time-Saving: With dropshipping, you don't have to handle product packaging, shipping, or fulfillment logistics. Your dropshipping supplier takes care of everything after you receive a customer order. This frees up your time to focus on marketing your products, managing your Amazon store, and providing excellent customer service.

Disadvantages:

Lower Profit Margins: Since dropshipping suppliers handle multiple aspects of the product journey, they typically charge higher per-item fees compared to bulk buying from wholesalers or manufacturers. This can lead to lower profit margins for you.

Less Control over Quality & Shipping: You relinquish some control over product quality and shipping times with dropshipping. Reliance on a third-party supplier means you might encounter issues like inconsistent product quality or longer shipping times, which can negatively impact customer satisfaction.

Limited Branding Opportunities: With dropshipping, you might have less control over product packaging or branding materials. This can make it challenging to differentiate your brand from competitors who might be selling the same dropshipped products.

Example: Imagine you've identified a rising trend for fidget toys

However, you'll need to be mindful of the potential downsides. The dropshipping supplier might charge higher per-item fees, potentially reducing your profit margin. Additionally, you might have limited control over the quality of the fidget toys or the shipping times, which could impact customer experience.

Dropshipping can be a suitable option for new sellers or those with limited capital, especially for testing product ideas. However, carefully consider the potential drawbacks and ensure you partner with a reliable dropshipping supplier known for quality products and efficient fulfillment processes.

Choosing the right product sourcing option is a critical decision for Amazon entrepreneurs, influencing both short-term success and long-term sustainability. Carefully assess your business goals, budget, and desired level of control before making a decision. Whether opting for manufacturers, wholesalers, print on demand, or dropshipping, each method comes with its unique advantages and challenges.

By now, you've armed yourself with powerful product research techniques and explored various sourcing options. Did you identify the right model to find a profitable product with strong demand and the potential to generate healthy margins on Amazon?

Product research is the foundation of your Amazon business. Choosing the right product can be the difference between a wildly successful venture and one that quietly fizzles out. In this chapter, we'll strip away the mystery around product research and break it into clear, actionable steps. You'll learn how to evaluate what makes a product profitable, how to assess market demand and competition, the best tools to streamline your research, and how to avoid traps that catch many new sellers. By the end, you'll not only know how to find great product opportunities - you'll know how to assess them like a pro.

WHAT MAKES A PRODUCT PROFITABLE?

When you hear the word 'profitable', you may think of the final number in your bank account. But profitability in Amazon FBA is nuanced. There are multiple layers of costs and metrics to consider.

1. High Perceived Value, Low Cost

You want a product that can command a strong price in the marketplace while being inexpensive to source. A £20-£40 product that costs £3-£8 to manufacture and ship is the sweet spot.

2. Low Competition (But Not Zero)

Some competition means there's a market, but too much can lead to a pricing war. You're looking for gaps - niches that are active but underserved.

3. Lightweight & Small

Lower shipping costs = higher profit. Look for products under 1.5kg that can fit in a shoebox. Avoid oversized or bulky items unless your margins are very high.

4. Durable & Simple

Fragile products lead to high return rates and negative reviews. Avoid electronics or anything with moving parts unless you're confident in manufacturing.

5. Recurring Demand

You want evergreen products - items people buy year-round - not seasonal fads. Think kitchen accessories, pet products, fitness gear, and home organisation tools.

6. Room for Differentiation

If you can't improve the product or offer better branding, you'll be stuck competing only on price. Unique colours, better materials, bundling, or solving a minor problem can help you stand out.

UNDERSTANDING MARKET DEMAND & COMPETITION

A product isn't profitable if no one wants it, even if it has great margins. Likewise, even hot products can be too competitive. Here's how to evaluate demand and competition:

Step 1: Search Volume

Use tools like Helium 10, Jungle Scout, or AMZScout to check how many people are searching for the product or related keywords on Amazon every month. A good target: 3,000-15,000 searches/month per main keyword.

Step 2: Sales Volume

Look at the estimated monthly sales of top-ranking products. If the top 10 listings in a niche all do 500+ sales a month, that indicates strong demand.

Step 3: Revenue Spread

You want to see revenue distributed across several listings - not just one dominating the niche. If a single listing gets 90% of the sales, you'll have a tough time entering the market.

Step 4: Review Depth

Are the top sellers all sitting above 2,000 reviews? That's tough. Look for niches where you can compete at 100-300 reviews.

Step 5: Price Consistency

If everyone in the niche is charging roughly the same price, it's a stable market. If prices vary wildly, it could indicate customer confusion or low perceived value.

TOOLS AND TRICKS FOR RESEARCHING IDEAS

Technology has made product research more accessible than ever. Here are the top tools and some little-known tricks that can help:

1. Helium 10

This is the gold standard for Amazon product research. Use the Black Box feature to filter by sales volume, price, review count, weight, and more.

- *Cerebro: Reverse-search ASINs to see all the keywords a product ranks for.*
- *Xray (Chrome Extension): Run on any search results page to see estimated sales, pricing, and reviews.*

2. Jungle Scout

Another industry giant. Use Product Database and Product Tracker to find and monitor potential products. Great for validating trends.

3. Google Trends

Check seasonality and trend spikes. A product trending up in Google often reflects growing interest.

4. EcomCrew Niche Rater

Great for idea inspiration and assessing whether a niche has good fundamentals.

5. Alibaba and AliExpress

Check sourcing costs and find suppliers. If you see a product for £3 that sells for £25, you're onto something.

6. Amazon's 'Customers Also Bought' and 'Frequently Bought Together'

These sections offer insights into bundling ideas and related product niches.

AVOIDING PRODUCTS THAT SEEM GREAT (BUT LOSE MONEY)

Many new sellers fall into traps because a product "looks" like a winner. Here are red flags to watch out for:

1. Patent Issues

Never sell a patented product. Use Google Patent Search and consult professionals if unsure.

2. High Return Rates

Some products look profitable but generate huge returns - clothing, electronics, fragile items, etc.

3. Brand Dominance

Avoid categories where big brands like Nike or Apple dominate. You won't win on name recognition.

4. Price Wars

If sellers are consistently dropping prices and undercutting each other, margins will evaporate fast.

5. Misleading Data

Some tools overestimate sales. Always cross-check with multiple tools or monitor a product manually for a few weeks.

6. Seasonal or Fad Items

Don't build your business on products like fidget spinners Halloween decorations, or Christmas sweaters. These spike and crash.

EXERCISE & ACTIVITY

THE 10 POINT PRODUCT CHECKLIST

Before choosing any product, run it through this checklist:

1. *Lightweight and small (under 1.5kg, fits in a shoebox)*
2. *Sell for £20 - £50*
3. *Costs less than 25% of the sale price to source*
4. *Consistent monthly search volume over 3000*
5. *Review competition under 500*
6. *Not patented*
7. *Evergreen (not seasonal)*
8. *Simple, not prone to damage*
9. *Can be improved or bundled*
10. *No dominant brand*

If you can check off 8 or more, it's likely worth deeper research.

ACTIVITY

Take 30 minutes and complete this activity:

1. ***Go to Amazon and pick a category you're interested in.***
2. ***Look at the top 20 listings. Use the Helium 10 Xray tool or Jungle Scout extension.***

3. ***Write down the average price, review count, and estimated sales for top listings.***
4. ***Look for gaps: Are there listings with low reviews but high sales? Are customers complaining in reviews about the same things?***
5. ***Check Alibaba to estimate sourcing costs.***
6. ***Rank the product idea 1-10 on profitability, competition, and improvement potential.***

Repeat this weekly for 5-10 products. Patterns will emerge. That's your niche speaking to you.

FINAL THOUGHTS

Product research doesn't have to be overwhelming. It's a mix of data, intuition, and experimentation. Your goal isn't to find a perfect product it's to find a viable one that you can improve, brand, and market well.

Trust the process. Trust the numbers. And most of all, trust that with the right strategy, your first (or next) product could be the start of something amazing.

In the next chapter, we'll dive into branding and how to position your product, so it commands attention, builds trust, and earns loyalty.

Your product research journey starts now go explore!

PART 2
MASTERING AMAZON BASICS

CHAPTER 5:
SOURCING YOUR FIRST PRODUCT

Sourcing your first product can feel like a major leap forward – and it is. This is where your business starts to take physical shape. Until now, you may have done research, explored product opportunities, and envisioned your brand. But choosing a supplier and ordering that first sample? That's the first real step toward bringing your product to life.

In this chapter, we will cover how to confidently find the right supplier, evaluate product quality, and navigate shipping logistics without getting overwhelmed. Whether you're looking to import products from overseas or source locally, this guide is your roadmap.

WHERE TO FIND RELIABLE SUPPLIERS (DOMESTIC & OVERSEAS)

Your first big decision is where to source your product. Generally, you have two main options:

- ***Domestic Suppliers (based in your home country)***

- ***Overseas Suppliers (primarily in countries like China, India, Vietnam, etc.)***

1. Domestic Suppliers

Domestic suppliers offer several advantages:

- ***Faster shipping times***
- ***Easier communication***
- ***No import duties/customs issues***
- ***Better perceived quality (sometimes)***

However, they tend to be more expensive. For many new sellers, the higher cost of production might make local sourcing less attractive.

Where to Find Them:

- ***ThomasNet (US)***
- ***Makers Row***
- ***UKManufacturing.co.uk (for UK sellers)***
- ***Trade shows***
- ***Local directories***
- ***LinkedIn and business forums***

2. Overseas Suppliers

China is the most common country for sourcing due to its manufacturing scale and low costs. However, many sellers are now exploring India, Vietnam, Pakistan, and Mexico as alternatives.

Pros:

- ***Lower production costs***
- ***Wide product variety***
- ***Flexible Minimum Order Quantities (MOQs)***

Cons:

- ***Longer lead times***
- ***Language/cultural barriers***
- ***Higher risk of quality issues***
- ***Must deal with customs and import duties***

Where to Find Them:

- ***Alibaba.com (most popular)***
- ***GlobalSources.com***
- ***DHGate.com (smaller orders)***
- ***1688.com (requires agent or translation)***

Pro Tip:

Start with Alibaba. It's user friendly and includes Trade Assurance, which gives you some protection.

ORDERING SAMPLES AND CHECKING QUALITY

Never, ever skip the sampling stage.

Even if your supplier looks great on paper, a sample tells you how the product actually looks, feels, and functions, and whether it aligns with your expectations.

Why You Need a Sample:

- *Verify quality*
- *Inspect branding options*
- *Test durability, packaging, and functionality*
- *Catch issues before placing a large order*

How to Order a Sample:

1. *Choose three to five potential suppliers.*
2. *Contact each one with a short, professional message. Ask about price, Minimum Order Quantities (MOQs), customization and lead time.*
3. *Ask for a sample and be willing to pay for shipping.*

Sample Evaluation Checklist:

- *Is the product well made?*
- *Does it match the product listing?*
- *How's the packaging?*
- *Are there any safety concerns?*
- *Are you proud to put your brand on it?*

Take notes. Keep the sample. This becomes your benchmark.

Pro Tip:

Order from multiple suppliers and compare. This will give you leverage when negotiating.

BASICS OF SHIPPING, CUSTOMS & COSTS

Shipping might seem complex, but you don't need to be a freight expert to get started. Here's what you should understand.

Key Shipping Terms:

- *FOB (Free on Board): Supplier pays to get goods to the port. You pay from there.*
- *EXW (Ex Works): You handle shipping from the factory door.*
- *DDP (Delivered Duty Paid): You pay upfront; supplier delivers all the way to your door.*

For beginners, DDP or FOB is usually the safest route.

Shipping Methods:

- *Air Express (DHL, FedEx, UPS): Fast, expensive, great for small shipments/samples.*
- *Air Freight: Slower than express, cheaper for medium weight.*
- *Sea Freight: Best for bulk. Slow but very cost-effective.*

Customs & Duties:

- *Use a freight forwarder or customs broker*
- *Ask your supplier for the HS Code to estimate duties*
- *Each country has its own import tax thresholds*

Tool:

Use SimplyDuty or EasyShip for import tax calculators.

EXERCISE & ACTIVITY

FIRST TIME SELLER'S CHECKLIST BEFORE YOU ORDER

Before placing your first big order, go through this checklist:

1. Product Validation

Have you confirmed market demand?

Did you analyse your competition?

2. Supplier Verification

Are they a Gold Supplier on Alibaba?

Do they respond promptly and professionally?

3. Sample Evaluation

Does the product meet quality expectations?

Do you have clear photos and notes?

4. Contract Terms

Have you agreed on lead times, price, shipping method?

Do you have everything in writing?

5. Production Quantity

Are you ordering the MOQ, or did you negotiate a test order?

6. Branding & Packaging

Are you doing private label?

Did you provide your logo, design files, or custom instructions?

7. Shipping Method

Are you clear on who handles shipping?

Have you chosen air or sea?

8. Import Rules

Did you check customs duties and taxes?

Is your product restricted in your country?

9. Payment Terms

Are you using secure methods? (PayPal, Alibaba Trade Assurance, or Escrow)

Are you splitting payment (E.g.,, 30% deposit, 70% before shipping)?

10. Backup Plan

Do you have a second supplier identified in case of issues?

SUPPLIER COMPARISON MATRIX

Create a spreadsheet with the following columns:

- ***Supplier Name***
- ***MOQ***
- ***Unit Cost***
- ***Sample Cost***
- ***Communication Quality (1-5)***
- ***Shipping Time***
- ***Branding Options***
- ***Notes***

Score each supplier and choose the best.

Final Thoughts: Sourcing is a skill. Your first sourcing experience might feel uncertain. You'll second-guess yourself. You'll wonder if you're being scammed. You might obsess over minor details.

That's normal.

But like any skill, sourcing gets easier with experience. After your first order, you'll gain confidence. You'll learn how to spot red flags, negotiate effectively, and set better expectations.

Start small. Keep records. Build strong relationships with good suppliers. And remember: product quality is the bedrock of your brand.

Your first order is more than just boxes in a container. It's the beginning of something you built.

Let's move on to the next chapter, where we get your product ready for the world.

PART 3
SELLING ON AMAZON

CHAPTER 6:
CREATING LISTINGS THAT ACTUALLY SELL

Imagine a captivating storefront window that entices customers to step inside and explore. That's exactly what your Amazon product listing needs to be - a compelling magnet that draws in potential buyers and converts them into loyal customers.

In this chapter, we'll delve into the art of crafting high-quality product listings that showcase your products in the best light possible, ultimately boosting your sales and propelling your Amazon business forward. So, let's get started on building your conversion machine!

WHAT IS A PRODUCT LISTING AND WHY DOES IT MATTER?

Your Amazon product listing is essentially your digital salesperson. It's the first impression potential customers have of your product, and it plays a critical role in influencing their purchase decision.

Look at this scenario you walked into a brick-and-mortar store overflowing with products. You approach a shelf teeming with similar items, each vying for your attention. Suddenly, a particular product catches your eye – the packaging is sleek, the information clear and concise, and the overall presentation sparks your interest. Congratulations! That product has mastered the art of the silent salesperson – the product listing.

In the dynamic world of eCommerce, your Amazon product listing takes centre stage. It's your digital storefront, the persuasive voice that converts curious clicks into confirmed purchases. Here's why a well-crafted product listing is vital for your Amazon selling success:

The All-Seeing Eye of the Customer: In the absence of a physical product to hold and examine, your listing is the customer's window into your offering. High-quality product images, informative descriptions, and clear specifications paint a vivid picture, allowing customers to make informed decisions.

The Power of Persuasion: A compelling product listing doesn't just inform; it entices. By highlighting the product's benefits and addressing potential customer pain points, you craft a persuasive narrative that convinces customers why they need this product in their lives.

Standing Out from the Crowd: The Amazon marketplace is a vast sea of products. An optimised listing, incorporating relevant keywords and SEO best practices, ensures your product surfaces in relevant searches and grabs customer attention amidst the competition.

The Climb to Conversion Mountain: A well-structured listing, featuring clear calls to action, guides customers effortlessly through the purchase journey. By simplifying the buying process and removing any roadblocks, you nudge them towards that coveted 'Add to Cart' click.

A well-crafted listing provides all the necessary information buyers need to understand the product's value proposition and why they should choose it.

Here's why optimising your product listing is crucial:

Increased Visibility: By incorporating relevant keywords throughout your listing, you improve your product's ranking in Amazon search results, making it easier for customers to find you.

Enhanced Conversions: A compelling listing with high-quality images and informative descriptions entices potential buyers, ultimately leading to more sales.

Reduced Customer Returns: Clear and detailed information helps set expectations and avoids misunderstandings, minimising returns due to product misrepresentation.

Optimising Titles, Descriptions, and Bullet Points using relevant keywords. The power of keywords: Optimising your listing for search. Keywords are the building blocks of a successful Amazon product listing. They are the search terms customers use to find products on Amazon. By strategically incorporating relevant keywords throughout your listing, you increase your product's visibility and attract potential buyers actively searching for similar items.

Here's a breakdown of how to optimise each element of your listing:

PRODUCT TITLE:

- *Keep it concise (around 80 characters) and informative.*
- *Add your main keyword at the beginning of the title.*
- *Highlight key product features and benefits.*
  E.g., Wireless Noise Cancelling Headphones with Long Battery Life.

PRODUCT DESCRIPTION:

- *Provide a detailed and engaging description that goes beyond simply listing features.*
- *Use a mix of relevant keywords naturally throughout the text.*
- *Highlight the product's benefits and how it solves customer problems.*
- *Use bullet points to break up the text and improve readability.*

BULLET POINTS:

- *Use clear and concise bullet points to showcase the product's most important features and benefits.*
- *Use strong action verb at the beginning of each bullet point.*
- *Avoid keyword stuffing by including relevant keywords.*
- *Remember, the goal is to create informative and engaging content that speaks directly to your target audience's needs.*

Some Tips for Keyword Research Includes:

- *Use Amazon Seller Central's Keyword Research Artificial Intelligence tool.*
- *Analyse competitor listings to see which keywords they are using.*
- *Consider using keyword research tools like Jungle Scout (not affiliated with Amazon) for a more in-depth analysis.*

THE POWER OF PICTURES: CREATING HIGH-RESOLUTION PRODUCT IMAGES

In the digital world, high-quality product images are essential for grabbing attention and showcasing your product's features in detail. Unlike a physical store where customers can hold and examine products, high-quality images on your Amazon listing are your only chance to create a positive first impression. Think of them as captivating visuals that entice customers, highlight product features, and ultimately convince them to click 'Add to Cart.' Let's delve deeper into the importance of professional-quality product images and explore best practices for creating visuals that convert:

Professional Image Quality: Aim for crisp, clear images with good lighting and a clean background (ideally white). Customers will be turned off by distorted or blurry visuals.

Why Professional Images Matter:

The Power of First Impressions: In the digital realm, first impressions happen in milliseconds. Customers scrolling through search results make split-second decisions based on what they see. Professional images showcasing your product in its best light instantly grab attention, generate interest, and encourage customers to click on your listing for a closer look.

Building Trust and Credibility: High-quality images convey a sense of professionalism and trustworthiness. Blurry, pixelated, or poorly lit photos can create a negative perception of your product and brand. Investing in professional photography or mastering product photography techniques demonstrates your commitment to quality and builds trust with potential buyers.

Highlighting Features & Benefits: Professional images allow you to showcase your product's features and benefits in a visually compelling way. Close-up shots can emphasise intricate details, lifestyle images can demonstrate the product in use, and multiple angles provide a complete 360-degree view. This visual storytelling helps customers understand the product's value proposition and how it can enhance their lives.

Boosting Conversions: Studies consistently show that listings with high-quality images outperform those with poor visuals. Professional product images can significantly increase click-through rates, conversion rates, and ultimately, your sales.

CRAFTING SH*T HOT PRODUCT IMAGES

A Step-by-Step Guide:

Lighting is King: Ensure proper lighting is the foundation for your product photography. Natural daylight is ideal, but if using artificial lighting, opt for diffused light sources to avoid harsh shadows.

Main Image: This is the first image customers will see in search results, so make it count! Choose an image that is clear, eye-catching, and accurately represents your product.

Clean Backgrounds are Key: Distract clutter is the enemy! Use a clean, white background to make your product the star of the show. This allows for clear product visibility and emphasises its features.

Multiple Angles Matter: Don't leave customers guessing! Showcase your product from multiple angles including front, back, sides, top, and bottom. Consider including close-up shots of key features or intricate details.

Lifestyle Images: Consider including lifestyle images that demonstrate how your product is used in real-life settings. This helps customers visualize themselves using the product and enhances its appeal.

Highlight Functionality: Go beyond static product shots. Consider incorporating lifestyle images that demonstrate the product in use. This helps customers visualise how the product integrates into their lives and its potential benefits.

Maintain Consistent Style: Strive for visual consistency across all your product images. Use the same background, lighting setup, and image editing style to create a cohesive brand identity on your Amazon store.

Scenario Examples: You're selling a sleek, stainless-steel travel mug.

Professional Image: The mug is photographed against a clean, white background. The image showcases the mug from multiple angles, including a close-up of the leak-proof lid. An additional lifestyle image depicts someone using the mug while walking.

Image Source: Amazon

By prioritising professional-quality product images, you transform your Amazon listings into visually compelling storefronts that captivate customers, boost conversions, and propel your e-commerce business to new heights!

Additional Tips:

- ***Use a high-resolution camera (or smartphone with a good camera) and proper lighting.***
- ***Edit your images for brightness, contrast, and colour balance, but avoid excessive editing.***
- ***Optimise image file size for faster loading times on Amazon.***
- ***Follow Amazon's image guidelines to ensure your images meet their specifications.***

By investing in high-quality product images, you'll create a visually compelling listing that showcases your product's value and increases your conversion rates.

TAKING YOUR LISTINGS TO THE NEXT LEVEL

A+ CONTENT

You've mastered the art of crafting compelling product listings - fantastic! But what if you could elevate your Amazon game even further and create product descriptions that truly captivate customer attention? Enter A+ Content, an optional yet powerful tool offered by Amazon that empowers you to craft richer, more engaging product descriptions.

Think of A+ Content as supercharged product descriptions on steroids. It goes beyond the basic bullet points and text to incorporate high-resolution images, charts, infographics, and even video content. This enhanced visual storytelling allows you to showcase your product's features and benefits in a way that static text simply can't achieve.

The Benefits of A+ Content:

Enhanced Storytelling: A+ Content lets you weave a captivating product narrative. By incorporating compelling visuals and descriptive text, you can explain complex features, showcase product benefits in action, and create an emotional connection with potential customers.

Increased Engagement: Eye-catching visuals are proven to boost engagement. A+ Content with high-quality images, infographics, and even short product videos grabs customer attention, keeps them scrolling, and encourages them to delve deeper into your product details.

Improved Conversions: Studies consistently show that A+ Content can lead to significant increases in conversion rates. Engaged customers who understand the product's value proposition are more likely to click "Add to Cart" and complete the purchase.

Brand Differentiation: A+ Content allows you to go beyond basic product information and showcase your brand story. You can incorporate brand logos, explain your manufacturing process, or highlight your commitment to sustainability – all within your product description. This sets you apart from competitors and strengthens your brand identity.

Examples of A+ Content Elements

High-Resolution Images: Showcase your product in stunning detail from multiple angles. Consider lifestyle images or close-up shots of key features.

Comparison Charts: Simplify complex product features by using easy-to-understand comparison charts. This is particularly helpful for products with multiple variations or technical specifications.

Informative Infographics: Use creative infographics to explain product benefits or highlight key features in a visually engaging way.

Compelling Video Content: Short product videos can be incredibly powerful. Consider including explainer videos, product demonstrations, or customer testimonials within your A+ Content.

Example:

Scenario: You're selling a premium line of organic skincare products.

A+ Content Example: Your A+ Content description might feature high-resolution images showcasing the beautiful packaging and natural ingredients. You could incorporate an infographic highlighting the product's key benefits for different skin types. A short video might demonstrate how to apply the products for optimal results.

While A+ Content is an optional paid service, it can be a valuable investment for sellers looking to take their product descriptions to the next level and significantly boost their conversion rates. By harnessing the power of visual storytelling and richer content formats, you can create Amazon listings that truly stand out from the crowd and propel your products towards e-commerce success!

While high-quality product listings are essential, Amazon A+ Content allows you to go above and beyond. It's a paid service offered by Amazon that enables you to create richer and more engaging product descriptions.

Important Note: While A+ Content offers significant advantages, it's important to remember that it is only available to brands with a registered trademark. Carefully consider your budget and weigh the potential return on investment before opting for A+ Content.

If you take these steps to build a strong product listing for your chosen product on Amazon, you've successfully built a solid foundation for your Amazon product listing.

Remember, crafting a successful product listing is an ongoing process. By continuously refining your approach and incorporating valuable insights, you can turn your Amazon listings into powerful conversion machines that drive sales and propel your business forward.

Image Source: Amazon

WHAT A PRODUCT LISTING IS: AND WHY IT MATTERS

Think of your product listing on Amazon as your salesperson. It doesn't take breaks. It doesn't sleep. It represents your brand 24/7 to customers from all around the world. A listing is more than just a few lines of text and a couple of photos. It's a storefront, a pitch, and often the first...and only... impression you get to make. So, getting this right is not optional, it is essential.

Your listing is made up of several key components: title, images, bullet points, product description, keywords, and (if eligible) A+ Content. Each of these pieces works together to answer three key customer questions:

1. *What is this product?*

2. *Is it right for me?*

3. *Can I trust this seller?*

An optimised listing not only makes your product look professional and trustworthy, it also directly influences whether someone buys from you or from a competitor. Amazon's algorithm (A9) uses your listing content to determine where you appear in search results, and customers use your listing to make split-second buying decisions. That means good copy + good SEO = more visibility and more sales.

WRITING TITLES, DESCRIPTIONS AND BULLETS THAT SELL

Let's break down how to craft each part of your listing so it sells, rather than just sits there.

1. Product Title

This is the single most important text on your listing. It has to serve two audiences: the customer and Amazon's search algorithm.

Best practices:

- *Put your most relevant keywords at the beginning.*
- *Keep it readable, not stuffed with keywords.*
- *Include the brand, key features, material, size, colour, quantity.*
- *Stay within character limits (usually 200 characters max).*

Example: Instead of: "Bluetooth Headphones" Try: "Noise Cancelling Bluetooth Headphones Over-Ear Wireless, 40H Playtime, Built-in Mic, for iPhone & Android"

2. Bullet Points (Key Product Features)

Bullet points appear near the top of the listing and are often the first place shoppers glance.

Tips for great bullets:

- *Use 5 bullet points, each highlighting a distinct feature.*
- *Start with a benefit in ALL CAPS, then explain it.*
- *Include keywords naturally.*
- *Focus on how it solves a problem or improves life.*

Example:

- *LONG-LASTING BATTERY: Enjoy up to 40 hours of uninterrupted playback on a single charge.*
- *COMFORTABLE FIT: Adjustable headband and memory foam ear cushions for all-day use.*

3. Product Description

This is your chance to tell a story, add personality, and connect emotionally.

Structure it like this:

- *Open with a benefit-driven paragraph.*
- *Use short sentences and formatting (HTML tags for bold, line breaks).*
- *Reinforce key features.*
- *Add a call-to-action.*

THE POWER OF KEYWORDS & SEO FOR VISIBILITY

A beautiful listing is useless if no one sees it. That's where keywords come in.

Amazon is a search engine. Like Google, it uses keywords to determine which products show up for what searches. Your goal is to include relevant keywords that match customer search behaviour.

Where to Use Keywords:

- *Product Title*
- *Bullet Points*
- *Description*
- *Backend Search Terms (in Seller Central)*

Keyword Tips:

- *Use tools like Helium 10, Jungle Scout, or AMZScout to find high-volume, low-competition keywords.*
- *Don't repeat the same keyword excessively.*
- *Use long-tail keywords. E.g., wireless headphones for working out.*
- *Include alternate spellings or regional terms.*

Backend Keywords: In Seller Central, you can add hidden search terms that don't show on your listing but help with search visibility. Use all 250 bytes available. No commas or repetitions needed.

PREMIUM PRODUCT IMAGERY & A+ CONTENT: STANDING OUT IN SEARCH

Product Images

People shop with their eyes. Your product photos must:

- *Be high resolution (at least 1000 x 1000 pixels).*
- *Show the product on a white background for the main image.*
- *Include lifestyle images (product in use).*
- *Use infographics to highlight features and dimensions.*
- *Tell a visual story of the product experience.*

Invest in professional photos or learn how to DIY with proper lighting and editing. Photos make or break conversions.

A+ Content (Enhanced Brand Content)

If you're a registered brand on Amazon, you can create A+ Content. This lets you add additional images, charts, comparisons, and storytelling below the fold of your listing.

Why A+ Content matters:

- *Increases conversion rates by up to 10%.*
- *Reduces returns by setting better expectations.*
- *Helps you stand out from competitors.*

Include in your A+ Content:

- *Brand story*
- *Feature comparison charts*
- *High-quality lifestyle imagery*
- *Unique value propositions*

FINAL THOUGHTS: LISTINGS THAT SCALE

A great listing isn't just about getting your first sale. It's about scaling to 100, 1,000, or 10,000 sales. An optimised listing creates a flywheel effect:

- *More sales = more reviews*
- *More reviews = more social proof*
- *More social proof = higher conversion rate*
- *Higher conversion = better ranking*
- *Better ranking = more traffic*

This chapter has given you the foundation. In the next chapter we'll dig into advertising on Amazon how to drive traffic to your listing and turn browsers into buyers.

Remember: You don't need to be perfect. You just need to be clear, helpful, and compelling. Your listing is your voice. Make it count.

EXERCISE & ACTIVITY

The Anatomy of a High-Converting Amazon Listing (Checklist)

1. Product Title

☐ *Includes primary keyword naturally*

☐ *Highlights main benefit or unique selling point*

☐ *Follows Amazon character limits and style guidelines*

2. Product Images

☐ *High-resolution main image with a pure white background*

- ☐ *Additional lifestyle images showing the product in use*
- ☐ *Infographic images highlighting features, dimensions, and benefits*
- ☐ *Images comply with Amazon image requirements*

3. Bullet Points

- ☐ *Each bullet starts with a benefit-driven keyword or phrase*
- ☐ *Focus on problems solved and emotional benefits*
- ☐ *Includes secondary keywords naturally*
- ☐ *Clear, scannable, and easy to read*

4. Product Description / A+ Content

- ☐ *Tells a compelling brand and product story*
- ☐ *Uses formatting (A+, bold, spacing) for readability*
- ☐ *Reinforces benefits, use cases, and differentiation*
- ☐ *Includes additional keywords without stuffing*

5. Keywords and SEO

- ☐ *Thorough keyword research completed (Helium10/AMZ Suggestion/ Google)*
- ☐ *Backend search terms filled with relevant phrases*
- ☐ *No duplicate keywords in backend fields*
- ☐ *Long-tail keywords included for additional ranking opportunities*

6. Pricing and Offers

- ☐ *Competitive price compared to top sellers*
- ☐ *Coupon or discount applied (if beneficial)*
- ☐ *Clear value justification through images and copy*

7. Reviews and Social Proof

- ☐ *Strategy in place for compliant review generation*
- ☐ *Negative review trends analyzed and addressed in listing copy*
- ☐ *FAQs added to remove buying objections*

8. Compliance and Accuracy

- ☐ *All claims accurate and legally compliant*
- ☐ *Product details (size, materials, compatibility) precise and clear*
- ☐ *Listing matches actual product to avoid returns*

PART 3
SELLING ON AMAZON

CHAPTER 7
PRICING, INVENTORY & FBA ESSENTIALS

Imagine crafting the perfect product, a hidden gem with the potential to dazzle the world. But what if your treasure remains buried, unseen by potential buyers? Effective inventory management and competitive pricing are the shovels you need to unearth your Amazon store's true potential, transforming it from a hidden gem into a thriving marketplace destination.

In this chapter, we'll discuss the art of setting the right price for your products and explore the world of Amazon fulfillment options, ensuring your products are readily available to meet customer demand.

UNDERSTANDING INVENTORY: THE LIFEBLOOD OF YOUR BUSINESS

In the dynamic world of e-commerce, inventory management is the art of maintaining the right balance. It's the lifeblood of your Amazon business, directly impacting your ability to fulfill customer orders, optimise profitability, and ensure customer satisfaction. Here's a detailed breakdown of what inventory management entails:

What is Inventory?

Simply put, inventory refers to all the products you have on hand at any given time. This encompasses everything from:

Raw materials: If you're a manufacturer or private label seller, this includes any materials needed to produce your finished products.

Work-in-progress (WIP): These are products currently in the production process, not yet ready for sale.

Finished goods: These are your completed products, ready to be shipped to customers after an order is placed.

THE IMPORTANCE OF INVENTORY MANAGEMENT

Having a substantial amount of inventory is crucial because too little inventory can lead to stockouts, missed sales opportunities, and frustrated customers and too much inventory ties up your capital, incurs storage costs, and increases the risk of products becoming outdated. Here are some reasons why effective inventory management plays a crucial role in your Amazon business success:

Ensuring Order Fulfillment: You never want to run out of stock and disappoint a customer by being unable to fulfill their order. Proper inventory management practices ensure you have enough products on hand to meet customer demand and avoid stockouts.

Optimising Profitability: Overstocking can tie up your capital in unsold inventory, while understocking can lead to lost sales opportunities. Effective inventory management helps you strike a balance, minimising storage costs and ensuring you have enough products to capitalise on customer demand.

Improving Customer Satisfaction: Fast and reliable order fulfillment is key to building customer satisfaction. By effectively managing your inventory, you can ensure timely order fulfillment and minimise the risk of delays or cancellations.

KEY INVENTORY MANAGEMENT CONCEPTS

Lead Time: The time it takes for a product to be manufactured, shipped, and delivered to your Amazon warehouse or fulfillment centre. Knowing your lead time is crucial for planning your inventory levels and ensuring you have enough stock to meet customer demand.

Stock Keeping Unit (SKU): A unique identifier assigned to each product variation in your inventory. This allows you to track individual items, monitor stock levels, and optimise your inventory management processes.

Minimum Order Quantity (MOQ): The minimum number of units you need to order from a supplier. Understanding MOQs is crucial when sourcing products, especially when dealing with manufacturers overseas.

Safety Stock: This is an extra buffer of inventory you maintain to mitigate potential issues like unexpected demand surges, delays in shipments, or product returns.

EXAMPLES OF INVENTORY MANAGEMENT STRATEGIES:

Demand Forecasting: Analyse historical sales data and market trends to predict future demand for your products. This helps you determine how much inventory to order and avoid overstocking or understocking.

Just-in-Time (JIT) Inventory: This strategy aims to minimise storage costs by receiving inventory only when it's needed to fulfill customer orders. This can be a viable option for established sellers with reliable supplier relationships and predictable sales patterns.

ABC Analysis: This method categorises your inventory based on its value and sales velocity (how quickly it sells). You can then prioritise your inventory management efforts, focusing on high-value, fast-selling products (category A) and potentially implementing different strategies for less valuable or slower-selling items (categories B and C).

By understanding the importance of inventory management and implementing effective strategies, you can ensure a steady flow of products, optimise your profitability, and keep your customers happy – all key ingredients for thriving in the competitive world of Amazon selling!

By managing your inventory effectively, you will be able to:

- ***Accurately forecast demand: This helps you determine how much inventory to order and avoid stockouts.***
- ***Monitor inventory levels closely: Regularly track your inventory to ensure you have enough products in stock to fulfill orders.***
- ***Set reorder points: Establish a minimum inventory level that triggers a reorder to prevent stockouts.***

SETTING A COMPETITIVE PRICE: A BALANCING ACT

In the bustling marketplace of Amazon, pricing your products competitively is an essential skill for attracting customers, driving sales, and ultimately, achieving business success. Striking the right balance is crucial – a price too high can scare away customers, while a price too low can erode your profit margins. Here's a detailed breakdown of the key factors to consider when establishing competitive pricing for your Amazon products:

1. Competitive Research: Understanding the Landscape

Know Your Competitors: Before setting your price, delve into competitor research. Identify the products similar to yours and analyse their pricing strategies. Use Amazon search functions and third-party seller tools like Jungle Scout or Helium 10 to gather competitor pricing data.

Consider the Spectrum: Don't just focus on the average competitor price. Analyse the range – the lowest and highest priced offerings for similar products. This gives you a better understanding of the market landscape and potential pricing strategies. Are there established brands with premium-priced products? Are there new sellers offering aggressive introductory prices?

Go Beyond Price: While price is a significant factor, it's not the only one. Consider competitor offerings in terms of quality, branding, product features, customer reviews, and fulfillment options (Prime vs. non-Prime). This holistic view allows you to position your product competitively.

Example: You're selling a stainless-steel travel mug with a leak-proof lid and double-walled insulation. Through competitor research, you discover similar travel mugs priced between £15 and £30. Some competitors offer basic, single-walled mugs with plastic lids at lower price points. Others focus on premium brands, insulated mugs with advanced features like temperature control, at higher price points. There's also a range of offerings in between, with varying materials, functionalities, and brand recognition.

2. Cost Analysis: Unveiling Your Bottom Line

Cost Breakdown: It all starts with understanding your costs. Factor in all the expenses associated with bringing your travel mug to market, including:

- ***Manufacturing costs per unit (if applicable)***
- ***Material costs (stainless steel, lid, etc.)***
- ***Packaging costs***
- ***Shipping costs (from supplier to you and to fulfillment centres)***
- ***Amazon fees (referral fees, storage fees, fulfillment fees)***

Don't Forget Hidden Costs: Factor in any additional costs you might incur, such as marketing expenses, potential returns processing, and customer service.

Example: Let's say your stainless-steel travel mug costs £7 to manufacture, £2 for materials, and £1 for packaging. Factoring in shipping and Amazon fees, your total cost per mug might be £12.

3. Profit Margin: Striking the Golden Ratio

Price for Profit: Your price should not only cover your costs but also generate a healthy profit margin. This allows you to reinvest in your business, grow your inventory, and stay competitive in the long run.

Profit Margin Goals: While profit margin goals will vary depending on your business model and industry, a 20%-30%

profit margin is a general benchmark for many Amazon sellers. However, it's important to consider your specific circumstances. If you're a new seller, you might be willing to accept a lower profit margin initially to gain traction and positive reviews.

Example: Considering your costs and a desired 25% profit margin, you might need to price your travel mug at around $16 to achieve your profitability goals. However, if you see an opportunity to capture market share by offering a competitive price point, you might adjust your pricing strategy and be willing to accept a slightly lower profit margin (E.g., 20%) to undercut competitors and gain initial sales.

4. Perceived Value: The Customer's Perspective

Balancing Price with Value: Your travel mug's perceived value plays a crucial role in customer buying decisions. Customers are willing to pay more for products they perceive as high-quality, durable, and offering superior functionality (E.g., leak-proof, temperature insulation).

Highlight Your Value Proposition: When setting your price, consider the unique selling points (USPs) of your travel mug.

Do you use high-quality, food-grade stainless steel? Does it have a lifetime warranty? Does it boast a unique design or colour options?

Emphasise these aspects in your product listing and marketing materials to justify your pricing.

Example: You might price your travel mug slightly higher than some competitors if you use high-quality materials, offer a lifetime warranty, and highlight its sleek design and temperature insulation properties. By emphasising these USPs, you can convince customers that your product offers superior value despite a potentially higher price point. Remember, assessing competitive pricing is an ongoing process.

FINDING THE PRICING SWEET SPOT:

There are varieties of pricing strategies you can employ on Amazon:

Competitive Pricing: Matching or slightly undercutting the competition's price can be effective for attracting customers, especially for new sellers.

Value-Based Pricing: Setting a price based on the perceived value your product offers to the customer. This strategy can work well for unique or high-quality products.

Premium Pricing: Positioning your product as a luxury item and setting a higher price point can be effective for targeting a specific customer segment.

Remember: You can also utilise automated repricing tools to adjust your prices dynamically based on market conditions and competitor pricing (note: these tools are not affiliated with Amazon and may incur additional fees).

FULFILLMENT BY AMAZON (FBA): A HELPING HAND

Imagine this: you've identified a hot-selling product, created a compelling listing, and customers are flocking to your Amazon store. Orders are pouring in, but a nagging worry creep in - how will you manage packaging, shipping, and customer service for all these orders? Fulfillment by Amazon (FBA) steps in as your knight in shining armour, offering a helping hand that frees you up to focus on growing your business

What is FBA?

FBA is a service provided by Amazon that takes the logistics burden off your shoulders. By opting into FBA, you essentially outsource your fulfillment operations to Amazon's well-oiled machine. Here's how it works:

Send Your Inventory to Amazon: You send your products to one of Amazon's strategically located fulfillment centres across the country.

Storage & Warehousing: Amazon takes care of storing your inventory securely in their fulfillment centres.

Order Fulfillment: When a customer places an order on your Amazon listing, Amazon's fulfillment associates pick, pack, and ship the product directly to the customer.

Customer Service: FBA also includes basic customer service functionalities. Amazon handles customer inquiries regarding order tracking, returns, and exchanges for FBA orders.

By opting into FBA, you essentially outsource your fulfillment operations to Amazon's extensive network of fulfillment centers.

Benefits of FBA:

Convenience: FBA frees you up to focus on other aspects of your business, like marketing and product sourcing.

Scalability: Amazon's vast infrastructure can handle high order volumes, allowing you to scale your business effortlessly.

Fast & Reliable Shipping: By leveraging Amazon's vast fulfillment network, you can offer fast and reliable shipping to customers, potentially including benefits like free two-day shipping for Prime members. This can significantly boost your conversion rates and customer satisfaction.

Increased Visibility: FBA products are often eligible for Amazon Prime benefits, giving them increased visibility in search results and potentially attracting more customers.

Customer Satisfaction: FBA helps ensure fast and reliable delivery, potentially boosting your customer satisfaction ratings.

Prime Badge Eligibility: Products fulfilled by Amazon are eligible for the coveted 'Prime Badge', increasing their visibility and attracting Prime members.

Drawbacks of FBA:

Costs: FBA incurs storage and fulfillment fees, which can impact your profit margins.

Less Control: You relinquish some control over the fulfillment process when using FBA.

Examples of How FBA Benefits Sellers:

Small Business Owner: Jane runs a home-based bakery, selling her delicious cookies on Amazon. FBA allows her to focus on baking and recipe development without worrying about packaging and shipping each order. This frees up her time to fulfill wholesale orders and expand her product offerings.

Large Toy Manufacturer: A toy manufacturer uses FBA to fulfill customer orders placed directly through their Amazon store. FBA's extensive network ensures fast and reliable delivery, keeping customers happy during peak holiday seasons when order volume surges.

Considering the FBA Fees:

While FBA offers significant advantages, there are associated fees. These fees cover storage, picking, packing, and shipping costs. Carefully analyse the FBA fee structure to determine if it aligns with your profit margins, especially for smaller or lower-priced products.

While FBA is a valuable tool for Amazon sellers, offering a convenient and scalable solution for order fulfillment, it is important to understand its benefits and drawbacks, you can decide if FBA is the right fit for your business model and help you streamline your operations, freeing up time and resources to focus on growth and success.

FBA might be a perfect fit if:

- ***You have a high product turnover and require efficient order fulfillment.***
- ***You want to leverage the benefits of the Prime badge.***
- ***You lack the resources or infrastructure to manage your own fulfillment operations.***

Before deciding on FBA, carefully consider the associated costs and weigh them against the potential benefits for your specific business model.

CREATING A SHIPMENT PLAN AND SENDING INVENTORY

Fulfillment by Amazon (FBA) simplifies your life as a seller by handling the storage, picking, packing, shipping, and customer service for your products. However, before Amazon takes the reins, you need to create a well-defined shipment plan and ensure your inventory adheres to their guidelines. Here's a breakdown of this important step:

UNDERSTANDING SHIPMENT PLANS

The Roadmap to Fulfillment: A shipment plan acts as a roadmap, informing Amazon about the products you're sending, their quantities, and the specific fulfillment centre they should be directed to. This ensures your inventory reaches the right location for efficient order fulfillment.

Benefits of Clear Planning: Creating a shipment plan offers several advantages. It helps Amazon optimise storage allocation within their fulfillment centres, streamlines the receiving process, and minimises potential delays. For you, it ensures clear communication and avoids confusion upon product arrival.

Creating a Shipment Plan in Seller Central

- ***Navigate to Inventory: Log in to your Seller Central account and navigate to the 'Inventory' section.***
- ***Select 'Manage FBA Inventory': Within the Inventory section, look for the option to 'Manage FBA Inventory'.This will display a list of your products currently enrolled in the FBA program.***
- ***Choose Products for Shipment: Select the products you're ready to send to Amazon fulfillment centres. You can choose them individually or use bulk selection options.***
- ***Initiate Shipment Creation: Once you've selected your products, click on the 'Send/Replenish Inventory' button. This will initiate the shipment plan creation process.***
- ***Specify Quantities and Destination: Carefully specify the quantity of each product you're sending and choose the destination fulfillment centre from the available options. Consider factors like product demand and shipping times when selecting the fulfillment centre location.***

- ***Review and Submit: Thoroughly review your shipment plan for accuracy, ensuring product quantities and destination centre are correct. Once satisfied, submit the plan for Amazon's approval.***

PREPARING YOUR INVENTORY FOR SHIPMENT

Comply with Amazon's Guidelines: Amazon has specific guidelines for packaging and labelling products intended for FBA fulfillment. These guidelines ensure efficient processing and prevent delays. Failing to comply can lead to rejected shipments or additional processing fees.

Packaging Essentials: Use sturdy, sealed boxes that can withstand transportation. Ensure products are securely packed with appropriate cushioning materials to prevent damage during transit.

Labelling Requirements: Each box in your shipment needs clear and accurate labels generated through Seller Central. These labels include product identification information, fulfillment centre destination details, and other essential data. Amazon's system uses these labels to track and manage your inventory upon arrival.

Example:

Scenario: You're an FBA seller of handcrafted leather phone cases. You've decided to send 50 units of your brown iPhone 13 case and 30 units of your black Samsung Galaxy S22 case to an Amazon fulfillment centre on the West Coast.

Shipment Plan Creation: Through Seller Central's "Manage FBA Inventory" section, you create a shipment plan specifying the quantities (50 brown iPhone 13 cases and 30 black Samsung

Galaxy S22 cases) and select the appropriate West Coast fulfillment centre as the destination.

Inventory Preparation: You carefully pack the phone cases in sturdy boxes, ensuring they are secure with bubble wrap or other cushioning materials. You then print the FBA labels generated through Seller Central and affix them to each box clearly.

By creating well-defined shipment plans and meticulously preparing your inventory according to Amazon's guidelines, you ensure a smooth and efficient journey for your products from your warehouse to Amazon's fulfillment centres, ultimately paving the way for successful order fulfillment and customer satisfaction. While FBA offers numerous advantages, it's not the only option:

Merchant Fulfilled Network (MFN): With MFN, you handle the picking, packing, shipping, and customer service for your orders. This method requires more effort and resources on your part but can be cost-effective for low-volume sellers or those with unique fulfillment needs.

HOW TO PRICE WITHOUT LOSING PROFIT

The Cost Trap

Too many beginners make the mistake of pricing their products based on what competitors charge - without understanding their own numbers. If you don't know your true cost per unit (including all associated fees), you could be selling at a loss and not even realise it.

THE ANATOMY OF A PROFITABLE PRICE

To calculate a sustainable, profitable price, you need to understand all the pieces involved:

1. Product Cost

This is what you pay your supplier for the item itself. If you're using Alibaba or a domestic manufacturer, this includes the cost per unit and any setup costs.

2. Shipping Cost

This includes shipping from the supplier to Amazon's warehouse (if using FBA), customs fees, duties, and freight forwarding costs. Even packaging materials count here.

3. Amazon Fees

More on this below - but know that Amazon takes a cut for every sale. Expect 15% referral fees and additional charges for FBA.

4. Marketing/Advertising Costs

You'll likely spend money on PPC ads or influencer marketing. Factor a conservative estimate here (E.g.,10-20% of your price).

5. Profit Margin

Your reward. Aim for a minimum 30% net margin after all costs. Less than that makes scaling harder.

THE PRICING FORMULA

Here's a simple approach to pricing:

(Product Cost + Shipping + Fees + Marketing) × 1.3 to 1.5 = Retail Price

For example:

- ***Product cost: £2.50***
- ***Shipping: £1.00***
- ***Amazon fees: £3.00***
- ***Marketing: £1.00***
- ***Total cost: £7.50***
- ***Target Price: £9.75 to £11.25***

If your target market supports that pricing, you're in business.

Understanding Amazon Fees

Amazon's fee structure can be confusing, but let's break it down simply.

1. Referral Fee

This is Amazon's cut for bringing you the customer. It ranges from 8% to 20%, depending on the category. Most products fall under 15%.

2. FBA Fees (if using Fulfillment by Amazon)

Covers picking, packing, shipping, and customer service.

- ***Based on size and weight.***
- ***A small item might cost £2.20.***
- ***A larger item might be £5.00 or more.***

3. Monthly Storage Fees

Amazon charges to store your products in their warehouse:

- ***Standard: ~£0.75 per cubic foot***
- ***Q4 (Oct-Dec): Higher, around £2.40 per cubic foot***

4. Long-Term Storage Fees

If products sit unsold for more than 365 days, you'll be charged additional fees. So don't overstock.

5. Optional Fees

- ***Labeling***
- ***Prep services***
- ***Removal/disposal***

INTRODUCTION TO INVENTORY MANAGEMENT

Even great products fail due to poor inventory management. Run out of stock, and you lose ranking and sales. Overstock, and you bleed cash on storage fees.

Key Inventory Terms

- ***MOQ (Minimum Order Quantity): The smallest batch a supplier will sell.***
- ***Lead Time: How long it takes from placing your order to Amazon receiving it.***
- ***Reorder Point: When you need to order more (before you run out).***
- ***Buffer Stock: Extra inventory to handle delays or sudden spikes.***

How to Manage Inventory as a New Seller

1. ***Start Small Don't order 1,000 units right away. Test with 100-300 if possible.***
2. ***Use an Inventory Spreadsheet or Tool Track your units, sales velocity, and reorder points.***
3. ***Monitor Daily Sales Velocity Use tools like Sellerboard, InventoryLab, or even Amazon's dashboard.***
4. ***Plan for Reordering If your lead time is 30 days and you sell 5 units/day, reorder when you hit 150 units.***

Reorder Formula: (Daily Sales × Lead Time) + Safety Stock = Reorder Point

FBA (Fulfillment by Amazon) EXPLAINED SIMPLY

What Is FBA?

Fulfillment by Amazon means you ship your inventory to Amazon's warehouse. When someone buys, Amazon picks, packs, ships, and handles returns. You just watch the orders roll in.

Pros of FBA

1. ***Prime Badge Your listings get the coveted Prime badge - which can boost conversions by up to 70%.***
2. ***Hands-Off Logistics No packing boxes, trips to the post office, or customer service hassles.***
3. ***24/7 Sales Amazon handles everything while you sleep or travel.***
4. ***Customer Trust Buyers trust Amazon's shipping and returns.***

Cons of FBA

1. *Fees It's not free. You'll pay for storage and fulfillment.*
2. *Storage Limits New sellers often have low storage limits. This grows as your performance improves.*
3. *Inventory Control Once your items are in Amazon's warehouse, getting them back or modifying them can be tricky.*
4. *Product Prep You must meet Amazon's requirements for labelling and packaging. If not, they'll charge you to fix it.*

Should You Use FBA or FBM?

- *FBA: Great for scalability, Prime access, and convenience. Ideal for most new sellers.*
- *FBM (Fulfilled by Merchant): Better if you want total control or are selling large, low-margin items.*

Many sellers start with FBA and experiment with FBM as they grow.

Before You Place That First Order: Checklist

1. *Confirm your pricing model covers costs and profit*
2. *Use Amazon's FBA calculator for accurate fees*
3. *Know your supplier's lead time*
4. *Order samples and test product quality*
5. *Create a basic inventory tracking system*
6. *Decide if FBA is right for your first launch*
7. *Read Amazon's FBA prep & shipping guidelines*

Final Thoughts: Building the Backend of a

Real Business

Your product may be exciting, but behind-the-scenes operations, pricing, inventory, fulfillment are what keep it profitable.

The sellers who win on Amazon don't just launch great products, they master their margins, plan their inventory, and harness FBA to scale faster.

In the next chapter, we'll explore how to launch, advertise, and gain traction in your first 30 days.

This is where the real momentum begins.

EXERCISE & ACTIVITY

Have you considered the following factors?

- ***Pricing strategy based on market research, product cost, and desired profit margin.***
- ***Fulfillment method (FBA or MFN) that aligns with your business needs and resources.***

Answering "Yes" signifies you've taken the initial steps towards establishing a sound pricing and inventory management plan for your Amazon business. Remember, refining your approach based on ongoing sales data and customer feedback is crucial for long-term success.

As you move closer to launching your first product on Amazon, three core components will determine your success or failure in the early stages: pricing, inventory, management and fulfillment. Each of these elements can make or break your profits and momentum.

This simplifies the complexity around pricing strategies, Amazon's fee structures, inventory planning, and explains one of the most powerful tools available to sellers Fulfillment by Amazon (FBA).

By now you'll know how to:

- ***Price your product to cover costs and generate profit.***
- ***Understand all the fees Amazon takes (so you're not caught off guard).***
- ***Keep inventory flowing so you don't run out (or over-order).***
- ***Decide if FBA is right for you (spoiler: it often is).***

Let's get to work.

PART 3
SELLING ON AMAZON

CHAPTER 8:

LAUNCHING YOUR PRODUCT & GETTING YOUR FIRST SALES

Launching a product on Amazon is a thrilling experience. I still remember my first sale! After weeks or even months of research, sourcing, product testing, and listing optimisation, it's time to bring your product to life and into the hands of customers. But this stage isn't just about hitting the 'publish' button on your listing. It's about understanding how Amazon works, leveraging the right tools, and executing a thoughtful launch strategy to gain momentum early.

This chapter will walk you through every critical step of launching your product successfully and getting those all-important first sales without burning your budget.

UNDERSTANDING THE AMAZON ALGORITHM

Amazon's search engine is powered by an algorithm commonly referred to as A9. It determines what products show up in search results when customers type in queries. Understanding how A9 works is foundational for any seller.

The Goal of A9

Amazon's goal is simple: show customers the products they are most likely to buy. A9 does this by evaluating various data points, including:

- ***Sales velocity - How often a product sells in a short period.***
- ***Keyword relevance - Whether your listing includes the words a customer searched.***
- ***Conversion rate - The percentage of people who view your listing and make a purchase.***
- ***Customer reviews and ratings - More positive feedback boosts trust.***
- ***Pricing - Competitive pricing increases attractiveness.***
- ***Availability - Products in stock get preference.***
- ***Fulfillment method - FBA products typically rank higher.***

To win at A9, your job is to optimise your listing and increase conversions while driving initial traffic to your listing.

PRODUCT LAUNCH BASICS (Step-by-Step)

Launching your product the right way can significantly influence its long-term success. Here's a clear roadmap:

Step 1: Final Listing Check

- ***Ensure title, bullets, description, and backend keywords are optimised***
- ***Upload high-quality images***
- ***Enable A+ Content if available***
- ***Double-check inventory is received and active in your FBA account***

Step 2: Set Launch Pricing

Temporarily lower your price to increase conversions and attract early buyers. This doesn't mean you lose money, you're investing in momentum. You can raise the price later.

Step 3: Enable Amazon PPC

Begin running Amazon Pay-Per-Click (PPC) ads immediately. Focus on:

- ***Auto campaigns to let Amazon test where you convert***
- ***Manual keyword campaigns based on your keyword research***

Step 4: Request Reviews

Use Amazon's 'Request a Review' button in Seller Central after each sale. You can also enrol in the Amazon Vine program (available to brands) to get early reviews.

Step 5: Monitor and Adjust

Track your:

- ***Click-through rates (CTR)***
- ***Conversion rates***
- ***Keyword ranking***
- ***PPC performance***

Optimise daily during your first few weeks. Identify what's working and adjust accordingly.

AMAZON PPC (ADVERTISING) MADE SIMPLE

Amazon's internal ad platform allows sellers to promote products in search results and on competitor listings. PPC is essential during launch.

Types of PPC Ads

1. ***Sponsored Products - Appear in search and product pages. Most common.***
2. ***Sponsored Brands - Banner ads that show your logo and multiple products (available after brand registry).***
3. ***Sponsored Display - Retargeting ads that appear on and off Amazon.***

Budgeting for Your Launch

A good rule of thumb: Allocate 25–50% of your unit profit toward initial advertising. For example, if your profit per item is £5, consider spending up to £2.50 per sale on ads.

RUNNING YOUR FIRST CAMPAIGNS

Start simple:

- ***Auto Campaign: Let Amazon test where you convert. Set a low daily budget (E.g., £10).***
- ***Manual Campaign: Bid on exact match keywords you researched. Use suggested bids or start conservatively.***

Monitor performance daily. Look at:

- *ACoS (Advertising Cost of Sale)*
- *Impressions and clicks*
- *Conversion rates per keyword*

Turn off poorly performing keywords and scale winners.

BUILDING MOMENTUM WITHOUT BURNING CASH

Launching doesn't have to mean losing money Here are smart ways to build traction without draining your budget.

1. Use Social Proof Tactics

- ***Offer discounts to friends and family in exchange for honest reviews***
- ***Ask them to search your keywords and buy your product to boost organic ranking (within Amazon's TOS)***

2. Leverage Social Media

- ***Share your product on Facebook, Instagram, Reddit, and relevant forums***
- ***Consider a small Instagram influencer campaign in your niche***

3. Create a Simple Landing Page

Use a free tool (like Mailchimp) to build a one-page site with your product and a button that links to your Amazon listing.

4. Email Your Network

Let your contacts know about your launch and ask them to check it out and leave an honest review.

5. Use Coupons and Lightning Deals

Amazon offers several promotional tools:

- ***Coupons - Eye-catching green tags in search results***
- ***Lightning Deals - Time-sensitive offers that drive urgency***

WRAPPING UP

Your launch doesn't need to be overwhelming. Focus on visibility, conversions, and gathering those early reviews. A strategic launch sets the foundation for long-term sales and ranking.

Next, we'll go deeper into managing reviews, customer feedback, and maintaining strong seller metrics so your product thrives after the launch phase.

Let's keep building your momentum.

You've meticulously crafted your product listing, optimised pricing, and ensured efficient inventory management. Now comes the exciting moment: launching your product on the vast Amazon marketplace! But how do you ensure your masterpiece doesn't get lost in the sea of offerings?

This chapter equips you with powerful strategies to not only launch your product successfully but also propel your Amazon business towards sustainable growth.

Product Launch Strategies: Sparking Initial Sales and Reviews

A well-executed product launch on Amazon can be the catalyst that propels your product towards long-term success. Those initial sales and customer reviews create a snowball effect, boosting your product's visibility, ranking, and ultimately, conversion rates. Here's a detailed breakdown of key strategies to employ for a powerful Amazon product launch:

PRE- LAUNCH STRATEGIES: BUILDING ANTICIPATION

Optimise Your Listing: This is your foundation. Ensure your product listing is compelling and informative, featuring high-quality images, clear descriptions, and relevant keywords to attract potential customers during the launch phase.

Run Targeted PPC Ads: Consider utilising Amazon's Pay-Per-Click (PPC) advertising platform to target relevant keywords and drive traffic to your listing before launch. This builds anticipation and attracts potential customers who might be interested in your product.

Leverage Social Media: Create a buzz on social media platforms like Facebook, Instagram, or TikTok. Share engaging content about your product, highlight its features and benefits, and run targeted social media ad campaigns to reach your ideal customer base.

Offer Pre-Launch Discounts or Promotions: Generate excitement and incentivise early adopters by offering pre-launch discounts or special promotions. This can be done through email marketing campaigns or social media announcements.

LAUNCH DAY STRATEGIES: CREATING MOMENTUM

Flash Deals or Lightning Deals: Consider Amazon's limited-time deal options like Flash Deals or Lightning Deals to generate a surge in sales and customer interest on launch day. These deals create a sense of urgency and can significantly boost product visibility.

Influencer Marketing: Partner with relevant social media influencers or reviewers to showcase your product to their audience. This can introduce your product to a wider customer base and generate positive word-of-mouth on launch day.

Email Marketing Campaigns: Reach out to your existing email list or subscribers with targeted launch day promotions or announcements. This keeps them informed and motivates them to check out your new product.

POST- LAUNCH STRATEGIES: MAINTAINING THE MOMENTUM

Customer Reviews are King: Encourage customer reviews by offering excellent customer service, responding promptly to inquiries, and potentially including a product insert with a polite request for feedback. Positive reviews build trust and credibility, influencing future buying decisions.

Optimise Your PPC Campaigns: Continuously monitor and optimise your PPC campaigns based on launch day data and customer behaviour. This ensures you're reaching the right audience and maximising your return on investment.

Consider Bundle Deals or Promotions: Create product bundles or promotions with complementary items to increase sales and average order value.

Analyse and Adapt: Keep a close eye on your product's performance metrics like sales data, conversion rates, and customer feedback.Use this data to identify areas for improvement and adapt your strategies to optimise your product's long-term success on Amazon.

Examples:

Scenario: You're launching a new line of organic protein bars.

Pre-Launch: You optimise your listing with high-quality product images, detailed descriptions highlighting the ingredients and health benefits, and incorporate relevant keywords like 'organic protein bar' and 'healthy snack'. You run targeted PPC ads on Amazon and leverage social media platforms like Instagram to showcase the protein bars and their delicious flavours. You offer a 10% pre-launch discount to email subscribers who sign up for notifications.

Launch Day: You secure a Lightning Deal on Amazon, significantly reducing the price of your protein bars for a limited time. You partner with a health and fitness influencer on Instagram to do a product review and giveaway. You send a targeted email blast to your subscriber list announcing the launch day deal.

Post-Launch: You actively solicit customer reviews by responding promptly to inquiries and including a friendly review request with your product packaging. You monitor your PPC campaigns and adjust keywords based on customer search patterns. You consider offering a bundle deal with your protein bars and a sugar-free beverage. You analyse your sales data and customer feedback to see which flavours are most popular and identify areas for potential improvement.

By implementing these comprehensive launch strategies, you can ignite your Amazon product, generate initial sales and reviews, and propel it towards long-term success in the competitive landscape of the Amazon marketplace! Here are some additional strategies to consider:

Promotional Offers: Run limited-time discounts or bundle your product with complementary items to attract initial buyers.

Giveaways and Contests: Generate excitement and buzz around your product launch by offering free giveaways or hosting contests.

BUILDING MOMENTUM WITH AMAZON PPC ADS

In the ever-competitive world of Amazon, where millions of products vie for customer attention, organic search ranking alone might not be enough to propel your listings to the top. This is where Amazon Pay-Per-Click (PPC) advertising enters the scene, offering a powerful tool to strategically target your ideal customers and significantly boost your product visibility.

What is Amazon PPC?

Imagine a bustling marketplace where vendors shout out their wares to attract customers. Amazon PPC is your digital bullhorn, allowing you to target specific keywords relevant to your products and display your listings at the top of search results or on relevant product pages. You only pay when a customer clicks on your ad, hence the term 'pay-per-click'.

How Does Amazon PPC Work?

Keyword Research: The foundation of a successful PPC campaign lies in keyword research. Identify relevant keywords that people may be searching for about products like yours. Consider long-tail keywords (more specific phrases) to target high-intent buyers.

Bidding Strategy: Once you have your keywords, you set bids - essentially the maximum amount you're willing to pay for each click on your ad. Amazon uses a bidding system to determine which ads are displayed in prominent positions.

Campaign Creation: You create targeted PPC campaigns using Amazon's Seller Central or Advertising Console. Here, you define your budget, target audience, and product listings you want to promote.

Ad Display: When a customer searches for a relevant keyword, your ad might appear in sponsored ad sections at the top or bottom of search results pages or or product pages for complementary products.

THE ADVANTAGES OF AMAZON PPC

Targeted Reach: Unlike organic search, where ranking can be unpredictable, PPC allows you to target specific customer segments actively searching for products like yours. This ensures your ads reach highly relevant audiences more likely to convert into sales.

Bidding Strategy: Set your bids (the amount you're willing to pay) for each keyword. Higher bids generally lead to higher ad placement.

Campaign Optimisation: Monitor your campaign performance and adjust your bids and keywords as needed to maximise your return on investment (ROI).

Increased Visibility: PPC campaigns can propel your product listings to the top of search results, grabbing customer attention and significantly boosting their visibility amidst a sea of competitors.

Improved Conversion Rates: By targeting relevant keywords and showcasing your products to high-intent buyers, PPC can lead to a significant increase in conversion rates (the percentage of visitors who make a purchase).

Measurable Results: Amazon PPC provides detailed campaign reports, allowing you to track performance metrics like impressions (ad views), clicks, and conversion rates. This data helps you to make an informed decision when optimising your campaigns for better results.

EXAMPLES OF HOW AMAZON PPC BENEFITS SELLERS

New Electronics Brand: A new brand selling noise-cancelling headphones launches a PPC campaign targeting keywords like 'wireless noise cancelling headphones', 'best headphones for travel' and 'top-rated headphones for music'. This ensures their ads reach potential customers actively looking for such products, increasing brand awareness and driving sales.

Organic Supplement Seller: A seller of organic protein powder uses PPC to target long-tail keywords like 'plant-based protein powder for weight loss' or 'sugar-free protein powder for muscle building'.This approach attracts customers with specific needs, leading to more targeted traffic and higher conversion rates.

Things to Consider with Amazon PPC

Keyword Research is Key: Investing time and effort into thorough keyword research is crucial for a successful PPC campaign.The right keywords will ensure your ads reach the right audience.

Campaign Optimisation: PPC is an ongoing process. Monitor your campaign performance, analyse data, and adjust bids and targeting strategies to optimise results and maximise your return on ad spend (ROAS).

By harnessing the power of Amazon PPC and implementing well-structured campaigns, you can target your ideal customers, significantly boost your product visibility, and propel your Amazon business towards long-term success!

Amazon Pay-Per-Click (PPC) advertising allows you to target your ideal customers and display your product listings at the top of search results for relevant keywords. While not a free strategy, PPC ads can be a powerful tool for driving targeted traffic to your listing and increasing its visibility. Here's a basic understanding of how Amazon PPC works:

PPC advertising requires careful planning and ongoing optimisation to ensure its effectiveness.

BEYOND ADVERTISING: EXPLORING ADDITIONAL MARKETING STRATEGIES

In the dynamic landscape of Amazon, while PPC advertising offers a powerful tool for targeted reach, true success hinges on a well-rounded marketing strategy. Here's a deeper dive into additional marketing techniques that can work alongside PPC to elevate your Amazon presence and propel your sales:

1. *Search Engine Optimisation (SEO): The Art of Organic Visibility*

Imagine your product listing as a storefront on a busy street. SEO is like painting a catchy sign and keeping the window displays enticing. It involves optimising your product listing for relevant keywords that potential customers might use to search for products like yours on Amazon. By incorporating these keywords strategically throughout your listing title, bullet points, description, and backend keywords, you increase your product's organic ranking in Amazon search results. The higher your ranking, the more likely customers are to discover your product amidst a sea of competitors.

Keyword Research: Similar to PPC, SEO also relies heavily on keyword research. Identify high-volume, relevant keywords that accurately describe your product and target various stages of the buying journey (informational, research, transactional). Tools like Jungle Scout or Helium 10 can be helpful for keyword research.

Keyword Integration: Once you have your target keywords, strategically integrate them throughout your product listing. Focus on natural integration - don't stuff keywords unnaturally.

Compelling Product Content: Beyond keywords, craft compelling product content that informs, engages, and convinces potential customers. Use high-quality images, clear and concise descriptions, and highlight unique selling points (USPs) to differentiate your product.

Example: You're selling a handmade bamboo yoga mat.

SEO best practices involve:

Keyword Research: Identifying relevant keywords like "eco-friendly yoga mat," "natural yoga mat," "bamboo yoga mat for hot yoga," etc.

Product Listing Optimisation: Including these keywords in your product title (Eco-Friendly Bamboo Yoga Mat for Hot Yoga & Pilates), bullet points (for example, 'Sustainable Bamboo Material', 'Provides Excellent Grip & Cushion'), and product description (highlighting eco-friendly aspects and suitability for hot yoga).

2. Social Media Marketing: Building Brand Beyond Amazon

Don't confine your marketing efforts solely to Amazon. Social media platforms like Instagram, Facebook, or Pinterest can be powerful tools for brand building and customer engagement. Here's how:

Showcase Your Products: Use high-quality visuals to showcase your products in action. Post lifestyle images or short product demonstration videos to capture attention.

Run Social Media Contests and Giveaways: Generate excitement and brand awareness by running contests or giveaways on social media. Encourage user-generated content by asking customers to share photos using your product.

Targeted Social Media Ads: Many social media platforms offer sophisticated advertising options. Consider running targeted ads to reach potential customers based on demographics and interests.

Example: You can leverage social media for your bamboo yoga mat by:

- ***Posting captivating photos of people using the mat in beautiful yoga studio settings or serene outdoor locations.***

- ***Running a giveaway where users enter by following your account and tagging a friend who might be interested in trying a bamboo yoga mat.***
- ***Targeting social media ads towards users interested in yoga, fitness, or eco-friendly products.***

3. *Influencer Marketing: Partnering for Credibility and Reach*

Influencer marketing involves collaborating with social media personalities or industry experts who have a dedicated following relevant to your target audience. Here's the power of influencer marketing:

Credibility and Trust: People tend to trust recommendations from individuals they follow and admire. Influencers can introduce your product to a new audience and build trust through their positive endorsement.

Increased Brand Awareness: By partnering with relevant influencers, you can tap into their audience and significantly increase brand awareness for your product.

Targeted Reach: You can collaborate with micro-influencers (those with a smaller but highly engaged following) in your specific niche to ensure your product reaches a targeted audience genuinely interested in what you offer.

Example: For your bamboo yoga mat, you could partner with yoga instructors or fitness enthusiasts who have an established social media presence and target audience interested in sustainable yoga products.

By implementing a well-rounded marketing strategy that combines PPC advertising, SEO optimisation, social media engagement, and strategic influencer partnerships, you can create a powerful synergy that propels your product listings to the top of Amazon search results, builds brand loyalty, and ultimately drives long-term success for your Amazon business!

Excellent Customer Service: The Cornerstone of Trust and Building Long-Term Loyalty

In the cutthroat world of Amazon, where millions of sellers vie for customer attention, exceptional customer service isn't a mere courtesy - it's the golden key that unlocks trust, fosters loyalty, and propels your business towards long-term success. Here's a detailed exploration of how to leverage customer service as a strategic tool to differentiate yourself from the competition and cultivate a thriving Amazon business:

1. The Power of Prompt Communication: Responding in a Flash

Imagine a customer reaches out with a question about your product, eager to make a purchase. Every minute they wait for a response chip away at their enthusiasm. Here's why prompt communication is paramount:

Seize the Sales Opportunity: Fast response times demonstrate attentiveness and professionalism, increasing the likelihood of converting a curious inquirer into a paying customer.

Address Concerns Before They Escalate: A prompt response can nip potential problems in the bud. By addressing concerns quickly, you can prevent minor issues from snowballing into negative reviews or customer churn (loss of customers).

Set Expectations and Build Trust: By consistently responding promptly, you establish a reliable communication pattern, setting clear expectations for customer service interactions and building trust with your customer base.

Examples:

Scenario 1: A customer sends a message inquiring about the size chart for a particular garment you sell.

Best Practice: Respond within 24 hours, ideally within a few hours, providing a clear and concise explanation of the size chart and offering additional assistance if needed.

Scenario 1: A customer receives a damaged product and sends a message with photos attached.

Best Practice: Acknowledge their message promptly, apologise for the inconvenience, and offer a swift resolution – a replacement product, full refund, or store credit (depending on your policy).

2. Professionalism & Helpfulness: Cultivating a Positive Experience

Make every customer interaction an opportunity to leave a great impression. Train your customer service agents (CSRs) to exemplify the following fundamental characteristics:

Courtesy and Empathy: Treat every customer with respect, acknowledging their frustrations and demonstrating a genuine desire to help.

Clear and Concise Communication: Use professional language, avoid jargon, and ensure your responses are easy to understand.

Problem-Solving Skills: Equip your CSRs with the knowledge and resources to effectively troubleshoot customer issues and provide viable solutions.

Examples:

Scenario 1: A customer expresses frustration over a delayed shipment.

Best Practice: The CSR acknowledges the customer's frustration, apologises for the delay, and proactively investigates the issue. They then provide the customer with a clear update on the expected delivery timeframe and offer expedited shipping options if available.

Scenario 2: A customer asks a detailed question about the technical specifications of a product you sell.

Best Practice: The CSR demonstrates product knowledge by providing a clear and informative explanation, using visuals or diagrams if necessary. They offer to connect the customer with a product specialist if the inquiry requires further technical expertise.

3. Active Listening: Understanding the Customer's Perspective

Effective customer service goes beyond simply providing answers. It's about truly understanding the customer's needs and concerns. Here's why active listening is crucial:

Identify the Root Cause: By actively listening, you can uncover the underlying reason behind a customer's complaint or inquiry. This allows you to address the issue at its core and prevent future recurrences.

Build Rapport and Trust: When customers feel heard and understood, they're more likely to be receptive to solutions and develop trust in your brand.

Tailored Solutions: By actively listening, you can personalise your customer service approach, crafting solutions that cater to the specific needs of each situation.

Examples:

Scenario: A customer leaves a negative review stating the product didn't meet their expectations.

Best Practice: Instead of immediately defending the product, the CSR reaches out to the customer directly. They actively listen to the customer's feedback, understand what aspects of the product fell short, and offer a solution like a partial refund or exchange for a more suitable product.

Scenario: A customer asks a seemingly simple question about product usage.

Best Practice: The CSR practices active listening to understand the customer's deeper intent behind the question. They may uncover that the customer is a new user and requires more comprehensive guidance, prompting the CSR to provide additional usage tips or instructional resources.

4. Transparency and Honesty: Building Trust Through Open Communication

In the age of online reviews and social media, where customer experiences travel fast, transparency and honesty are no longer just desirable traits for customer service – they're essential for building trust and fostering long-term customer loyalty on Amazon. Here's a detailed breakdown of why upfront communication, even when delivering unfavourable news, is crucial for your Amazon business:

The Power of Transparency:

Maintaining Trust: When you're upfront and honest with customers, even in difficult situations, you demonstrate integrity and build trust. Customers appreciate knowing they can rely on you for accurate information and fair treatment.

Managing Expectations: By being transparent about potential issues or limitations, you can effectively manage customer expectations and avoid future disappointment.

Building Rapport: Open and honest communication fosters a sense of rapport with your customers. They feel valued and respected, strengthening the customer-seller relationship.

Examples of Transparency in Action:

Scenario 1: A customer orders a product, but due to unforeseen circumstances, there's a delay in shipment.

Best Practice: Proactively communicate the delay to the customer via email or phone call. Explain the reason for the delay (E.g., stock shortage, shipping carrier issue) and provide a revised estimated delivery timeframe. Offer apologies for the inconvenience and express appreciation for their understanding.

Scenario 2: A customer inquiries about a product's warranty policy, but there's a limitation or exclusion they might not be aware of.

Best Practice: Clearly explain the warranty policy terms, highlighting both the coverage and any limitations. Don't downplay or sugarcoat any exclusions. Give the customer all the exact information they need to make an informed decision.

ADDRESSING UNFAVOURABLE NEWS WITH HONESTY:

There will be situations where you need to deliver unfavourable news to a customer, such as:

- ***A product going out of stock after an order is placed***
- ***An inability to fulfill a specific customer request***
- ***A delay in processing a return or exchange***

Here's how to navigate these situations with honesty:

Acknowledge the Issue: Don't shy away from the problem. Acknowledge the situation directly and apologise for the inconvenience it causes the customer.

Offer Solutions: Whenever possible, present solutions or alternatives. This could involve offering a substitute product, expediting shipping on a backordered item, or providing a full refund for an unavailable product.

Be Clear and Concise: Communicate the situation clearly and concisely. Avoid using jargon or technical terms that might confuse the customer.

Example:

Scenario 1: A customer orders a specific colour variation of a product, but you discover it's actually out of stock.

Best Practice: Acknowledge the stock issue and apologise for the inconvenience. Offer the customer the option to choose a different colour variation that is available, provide an estimated timeframe for when the desired colour might be restocked, or offer a full refund if neither option works for them. Be transparent about the situation and avoid making promises you can't keep.

5. *Going the Extra Mile: Creating Lasting Positive Impressions*

By prioritising transparency and honesty in all customer interactions, you establish yourself as a reliable and trustworthy seller on Amazon. This builds customer confidence, fosters loyalty, and positions your business for long-term success.

While meeting customer expectations is essential, exceeding them can leave a truly lasting positive impression and turn satisfied customers into loyal brand advocates. Some ways to go the extra mile includes:

Proactive Solutions: Anticipate Potential Issues

Identify Common Pain Points: Analyse customer feedback and identify recurring issues or challenges customers face with your product or service.

Offer Pre-emptive Solutions: Based on your analysis, develop proactive solutions to address these pain points. This could involve including helpful instructional materials with your product, offering complimentary troubleshooting guides, or anticipating frequently asked questions and including them in your product FAQ section.

Example: You sell a complex self-assembly piece of furniture. Going the extra mile would involve including a clear and concise assembly manual with multiple diagrams, offering instructional assembly videos online, and even providing a helpline for customers who encounter difficulties during assembly.

Personalisation: The Power of the Human Touch

Remember Customer Preferences: If you have repeat customers, consider taking note of their past purchases and preferences. This allows you to personalise future interactions.

Targeted Recommendations: Based on past purchases, recommend complementary products or accessories that might enhance the customer's experience.

Birthday or Anniversary Greetings: A simple birthday or anniversary email with a special discount code can add a personal touch and demonstrate that you value their business.

Example: A customer frequently purchases organic teas from your store. You could send them a personalised email recommendation for a new organic tea variety they might enjoy, or offer them a discount on a tea steeper accessory.

UNEXPECTED DELIGHTS: SURPRISE AND IMPRESS

Include a Small Gift: Consider including a small, complimentary gift with some orders. This could be a sample of a new product, a handwritten thank-you note, or a discount code for their next purchase.

Upgrade Their Shipping: For larger orders or loyal customers, consider offering a free upgrade to expedited shipping to show your appreciation.

Example: You sell handmade jewellry. A customer places a significant order. Going the extra mile would involve including a complimentary polishing cloth or a pair of earring backs with their purchase, demonstrating thoughtful consideration.

By implementing these strategies, you can transform customer service from a reactive function to a proactive tool that builds trust, fosters loyalty, and propels your Amazon business towards long-term success. Remember, in the competitive world of Amazon, exceeding customer expectations is the new standard for exceptional service.

Strategies to Foster Long-Term Customer Loyalty

In the ever-competitive landscape of Amazon, where a seemingly endless array of sellers vies for customer attention, simply making a sale is no longer enough. The key to sustainable success lies in fostering long-term customer loyalty - transforming one-time buyers into devoted fans who consistently return to your store and recommend your products to others. Here's a detailed exploration of strategies you can implement to cultivate customer loyalty and build a thriving Amazon business:

1. The Personalised Touch: A Human Connection in a Digital World

Imagine walking into a store where the staff greets you by name, remembers your preferences, and offers tailored recommendations. This is the power of personalisation in the digital age. Here's how to incorporate a personal touch on Amazon:

Address Customers by Name: When responding to customer inquiries or emails, address them by name whenever possible.

This small detail adds a human touch and makes the interaction feel less transactional.

Acknowledge Past Purchases: If a customer has a history of buying from your store, acknowledge their past purchases in future interactions. You could suggest complementary products or highlight new arrivals that might interest them based on their buying habits.

Birthday or Anniversary Greetings: A simple automated email with a birthday or anniversary greeting and a special discount code can go a long way in personalising the customer experience and demonstrating that you value their business.

Example: A customer frequently purchases organic teas from your store. When responding to their email inquiry, you could use a greeting like 'Hi Roseline', acknowledge their past purchases ('We see you're a big fan of our organic teas!'), and recommend a new organic tea variety they might enjoy based on their previous purchases.

2. Proactive Approach: Anticipating Needs and Going Beyond

Don't wait for customers to encounter problems before offering solutions. By adopting a proactive approach, you can demonstrate exceptional customer service and build trust. Here's how to be proactive:

Identify Common Pain Points: Analyse customer feedback and identify recurring issues or challenges customers face with your product or service.

Offer Pre-emptive Solutions: Based on your analysis, develop proactive solutions to address these pain points. This could involve including helpful instructional materials with your product, offering complimentary troubleshooting guides, or anticipating frequently asked questions and including them in your product FAQ section.

Provide Additional Resources: Don't just wait for customers to reach out for help. Offer additional resources that might benefit them, such as blog posts with helpful tips on using your product or informative videos with assembly instructions.

Example: You sell a complex self-assembly piece of furniture. A proactive approach would involve including a clear and concise assembly manual with multiple diagrams, offering instructional assembly videos online even before a customer request them, and anticipating potential difficulties by providing a helpline for customers who encounter problems during assembly.

3. *Rewarding Loyalty: Showing Appreciation for Valued Customers*

Loyal clients are the cornerstone of any successful business. Implement strategies to show appreciation and incentivise repeat business:

Loyalty Programs: Consider implementing a tiered loyalty program that rewards customers for repeat purchases. This could involve offering points redeemable for discounts, early access to new products, or exclusive promotions.

Exclusive Offers: Reward loyal customers with exclusive discounts or special offers not available to the general public. This makes them feel valued and entices them to return for future purchases.

Birthday or Anniversary Gifts: A small token of appreciation, like a free sample or discount code on their birthday or anniversary, can create a positive impression and strengthen customer loyalty.

Example: You sell handmade jewellery. A customer has placed several orders from your store over the past few months. You could reward their loyalty by offering them a discount on their next purchase, sending them a free polishing cloth or a pair of earring backs with their next order, or granting them early access to a new jewellery collection launch.

4. Feedback as Fuel: Listening, Learning, and Improving

Customer feedback is a goldmine of valuable insights. Actively solicit feedback through surveys, product reviews, or post-purchase emails, and use it to continuously improve your offerings and customer service:

Make Feedback Easy to Provide: Include clear and easy-to-access channels for customers to leave feedback, such as surveys after purchase or a dedicated feedback link on your product listing.

Actively Analyse Feedback: Don't just collect feedback - analyse it thoroughly to identify trends and areas for improvement. Look for patterns in customer complaints or suggestions.

Implement Improvements Based on Feedback: Demonstrate that you value customer feedback by taking action. Address recurring issues, improve product descriptions based on customer suggestions, or implement new features based on customer requests.

Remember that building trust and loyalty is a continual activity. By consistently exceeding customer expectations and demonstrating a genuine commitment to their satisfaction, you can cultivate a loyal customer base that will not only return for future purchases but also advocate for your brand through positive reviews and word-of-mouth recommendations.

Here are some additional tips:

Invest in customer service training: Equip your team with the knowledge and skills necessary to handle customer interactions effectively.

Utilise customer service metrics: Track key metrics like response time and resolution rate to identify areas for improvement.

Embrace technology: Leverage available tools and resources to streamline customer service processes.

By prioritising exceptional customer service and fostering a customer-centric culture within your business, you'll be well on your way to building long-term customer loyalty and achieving sustainable success on Amazon.

Now that you've grasped the importance of customer service and its role in building trust and loyalty. Remember the key to success on Amazon lies in continuous learning and adaptation. Stay updated with the latest trends and best practices, experiment with different strategies, and leverage the wealth of resources available to refine your approach and achieve your business goals.

EXERCISE & ACTIVITY:

By incorporating the strategies outlined in this chapter, develop your plan to:

- ***Launch your product and generate initial sales and reviews.***
- ***Market your product effectively using various channels (optional: including PPC advertising).***
- ***Provide exceptional customer service to build trust and nurture long-term customer loyalty.***

Launch Checklist

Note down what you will do before and during launch

Before Launch:

-
-

Launch Week:

-
-

You've equipped yourself with the essential knowledge and strategies to launch your product successfully and navigate the exciting world of Amazon. As you embark on this journey, remember that continuous learning, adaptation, and a customer-centric approach are key to achieving long-term success.

PART 3
SELLING ON AMAZON

CHAPTER 9:
GROWING WITHOUT OVERWHELM

Launching your first product on Amazon is a milestone worth celebrating. But what comes next is just as important: maintaining growth, managing day-to-day operations, and doing it all without losing your mind. Welcome to the phase where many sellers either build a long-term business or burn out trying. This chapter is all about growing smart - strategically sustainably, and with systems that support you.

KEEPING TRACK OF PROFITS VS EXPENSES

It's easy to get caught up in revenue numbers: those top-line figures can look impressive. But seasoned sellers know that what matters most is profit - the money that actually ends up in your pocket. If you're not tracking expenses, you're not running a business. You're running a very expensive hobby.

The Profit Formula

Profit = Revenue - (Cost of Goods Sold + Amazon Fees + Advertising + Other Expenses)

Let's break that down:

- ***Revenue: Your total sales.***
- ***Cost of Goods Sold (COGS): What you paid for the product, including shipping and customs.***
- ***Amazon Fees: Includes referral fees, FBA fees, storage, etc.***
- ***Advertising: Amazon PPC, external ads, influencer marketing.***
- ***Other Expenses: Software tools, photography, packaging, barcodes, etc.***

TOOLS TO TRACK FINANCES

1. ***Amazon Seller Central Reports: These offer a basic snapshot of your revenue and fees. Use the 'Payments' and 'Business Reports' tabs regularly.***
2. ***Spreadsheet Templates: For those who love control, building a custom spreadsheet helps monitor expenses and profit margins product-by-product.***
3. ***Software Tools:***

   Helium 10 Profits

   Sellerboard

   Xero (for full bookkeeping)

Pro Tip:

Update your profit tracker weekly. Don't wait until tax season to discover you've been operating at a loss.

HOW TO MANAGE RETURNS AND NEGATIVE REVIEWS

Returns and negative reviews are inevitable. Even the most beloved products get 1-star ratings. What separates thriving sellers from frustrated ones is how they respond

Understanding Amazon's Return Policy

Amazon has a customer-first return policy. Buyers can often return products without prior approval, and sellers are expected to accept those returns (especially with FBA) It can feel unfair, but remember: the same policy also encourages customer trust, which leads to more sales.

Reducing Return Rates

- ***Clear Descriptions: Make sure your listings don't oversell or mislead.***
- ***High-Quality Images: Include multiple angles, close-ups, and use-case scenarios.***
- ***Instruction Manuals: Add simple, visual guides in packaging to help customers use your product correctly.***
- ***Durable Packaging: Protect against damage in transit.***

Handling Negative Reviews

You can't remove a negative review just because it hurts your feelings. But you can take action:

- ***Respond Publicly: Use Amazon's 'Respond to customer' option to clarify misinformation and show professionalism.***
- ***Improve the Product: Consistent complaints? Fix them. Add FAQs to your listing to preempt confusion.***

- ***Request Removal (If Legitimate): If a review violates Amazon's guidelines (E.g., it includes hate speech or talks about delivery instead of the product), request a removal through Seller Central.***

TURNING BAD EXPERIENCES AROUND

Go above and beyond to make things right. If a customer is truly unhappy, offer a refund or replacement - even if Amazon won't force you to. Kindness can lead to updated reviews or loyal buyers.

Customer Service Basics That Lead to Better Reviews

Want more 5-star reviews? Focus on delighting your customers.

Core Principles

- ***Speed Matters: Aim to respond to messages within 24 hours (or faster).***
- ***Politeness Pays: Use friendly, professional language - always.***
- ***Solution-Focused: Don't argue. Apologise and solve.***

Automating Customer Service (Without Losing the Human Touch)

- ***Use Message Templates: For common issues like 'Where's my package?'***
- ***Use Software:***

  Jungle Scout's Review Automation

  FeedbackWhiz or Helium 10 Follow-Up for email sequences

Follow-Up Messages That Work

Send a message post-delivery (compliant with Amazon's terms) thanking the buyer and inviting feedback. Example:

Hi [Customer Name],

Thank you for your recent purchase! We hope you're loving your [Product Name]. If there's anything we can help with, feel free to reach out.

If you're happy with your purchase, we'd be grateful if you'd consider leaving a review. Your feedback helps our small business grow.

Thank you, [Your Brand Name]

Avoid These Mistakes:

- ***Never offer money or gifts in exchange for reviews (against Amazon policy).***
- ***Don't spam. One polite follow-up is enough.***
- ***Don't argue with upset customers.***

SIGNS YOU'RE READY TO LAUNCH MORE PRODUCTS

Once your first product is generating consistent sales and you're no longer panicking every time a return happens, you might feel tempted to expand. But how do you know if you're really ready?

Green Flags:

1. ***Profitability: Your first product is consistently profitable (not just breaking even).***
2. ***Inventory Flow: You're managing stock levels without constant sellouts or overstock.***
3. ***Customer Service is Systematised: You're not constantly drowning in messages.***
4. ***Cash Flow Exists: You have profits to reinvest, not just credit cards.***
5. ***You Have Time: You're not already overwhelmed with one product.***

CHOOSING YOUR NEXT PRODUCT

Avoid the temptation to chase trends unless you're fully confident in your sourcing, branding, and marketing skills. Instead:

- ***Launch a variation (colour, size, bundle) of your current product***
- ***Solve an adjacent problem in the same niche***
- ***Use your existing customer base to ask what they need next***

Scaling Tip:

Track your KPIs (key performance indicators). Examples:

- ***Conversion Rate***
- ***ACoS (Advertising Cost of Sale)***
- ***Units Sold per Day***
- ***Refund Rate***

Know your numbers. What gets measured gets managed - and what gets managed can scale.

SYSTEMS THAT HELP YOU GROW WITHOUT OVERWHELM

The secret to sustainable scaling isn't working more - it's systematising more.

Document Everything

Create SOPs (Standard Operating Procedures) for tasks like:

- ***Responding to customer messages***
- ***Reordering inventory***

- *Launching PPC campaigns*
- *Updating listings*

Use tools like:

- *Google Docs or Notion for SOPs*
- *Trello or Asana for task management*
- *Zapier for automations (E.g.,, syncing orders to spreadsheets)*

OUTSOURCING WISELY

Once you have repeatable tasks, outsource them. Start with:

- *Virtual Assistants (for customer service, data entry)*
- *Freelancers (for listing optimisation, design)*
- *Agencies (for PPC or external traffic)*

Don't outsource what you don't understand. Learn it first, then hand it off.

Final Words: Growth Isn't a Race

Amazon success isn't about launching 50 products or scaling to 7 figures in your first year. It's about building something solid, sustainable, and aligned with your life goals.

Your journey is uniquely yours. Don't compare your Chapter 9 to someone else's Chapter 30.

Celebrate the wins. Learn from the losses. Keep going.

In the next chapter, we'll talk about brand building, off-Amazon growth, and setting the stage for long-term eCommerce success.

Let's keep building.

EXERCISE & ACTIVITY

List below what ideas you have taken from this Chapter on how to grow your business in the future - after you have learnt the basics of course!

-
-
-
-

PART 4
BUILDING BEYOND AMAZON

CHAPTER 10:
FROM SIDE HUSTLE TO BUSINESS OWNER

BUILDING YOUR BRAND: MORE THAN JUST A LOGO

One of the biggest mistakes new sellers make is thinking branding means just having a nice logo and choosing pretty colours. While visual identity is a part of it, your brand is much deeper than that. Your brand is how people feel about your business. It's what they say about you when you're not in the room.

A true brand is built on:

- ***Consistency: In voice, packaging, messaging, and customer experience***
- ***Promise: What customers can reliably expect from you***
- ***Personality: Are you playful, professional, luxurious, or affordable?***
- ***Purpose: Why does your business exist beyond making money?***
- ***Experience: How people interact with your product and your service***

Why Brand Matters

As your store grows, your brand becomes your moat. Products can be copied. Prices can be undercut. But a brand a relationship with customers is hard to duplicate. Brands drive repeat business, word of mouth marketing, and trust.

Brands create long-term equity. When your product is out of stock, loyal customers wait. When your competitor is cheaper, they still buy from you. That's the power of a strong brand.

EXPANDING BEYOND AMAZON (SHOPIFY, TIKTOK & MORE)

You've built your foundation on Amazon arguably the best launchpad in e-commerce. But long-term, depending entirely on one platform is risky. Amazon can change its algorithm, suspend listings, or shift its fee structure overnight. So, once you have proof of concept (steady sales, positive reviews, reliable fulfillment), it's time to expand.

WHY DIVERSIFICATION MATTERS

- ***Risk Mitigation: You don't want your entire income dependent on a single platform.***
- ***Control: On Amazon, you rent space. On your own site, you own it.***
- ***Higher Margins: You can avoid Amazon's fees by selling direct.***
- ***Customer Data: Platforms like Shopify allow you to build an email list, retarget with ads, and deepen customer relationships.***

Channels to Consider

1. ***Shopify: Build your own branded store. Ideal for long-term brand building and customer retention.***
2. ***Walmart Marketplace: Less saturated than Amazon but growing rapidly. Especially strong in North America.***
3. ***TikTok: Powerful for influences and social selling.***
4. ***Etsy: Great for handmade, vintage, and digital products.***
5. ***Retail & Wholesale: With branding and packaging dialled in, you may even approach brick-and-mortar stores or distributors.***

Expanding doesn't mean abandoning Amazon. Think of it like investing. Amazon is your foundation. Other platforms are your growth.

LONG TERM THINKING: SYSTEMS, OUTSOURCING & AUTOMATION

If your goal is time freedom, not just financial freedom, you must start thinking in systems.

What Is a System?

A system is a repeatable, scalable way to do something. Systems reduce stress, human error, and wasted time. When you systemise your business, you create repeatable processes that others can run even without you.

Examples:

- ***A checklist for how you list new products***
- ***A template for customer service emails***
- ***A step-by-step process for your monthly financial review***

Outsourcing

You don't need to do everything yourself. In fact, doing so will hold you back. Smart sellers hire help long before they feel 'ready'.

Start with small, low-risk tasks:

- ***Product research assistants***
- ***Virtual assistants for customer service***
- ***Freelancers for graphics, listing copy, or SEO***

Automation Tools

The right tools can do the work of multiple people. Here are a few to explore:

- ***Inventory & Order Management: Sellbrite, InventoryLab, or RestockPro***
- ***Email Marketing: Klaviyo, Mailchimp, or ConvertKit***
- ***Ad Automation: Perpetua, Teikametrics***
- ***Accounting: QuickBooks, A2X, or Bench***

The goal isn't just to scale revenue. It's to scale peace of mind. If you build smart systems early, you'll grow without burning out.

YOUR NEXT STEPS TO REAL ONLINE SELLING SUCCESS

You've come a long way. From learning about Seller Central to understanding product research, sourcing, listing creation, launch strategies, and now thinking like a brand owner.

Here's what to do next:

1. *Audit Your Brand*

   Do you have a clear brand voice?

   Is your packaging memorable?

   Do customers know what you stand for?

2. *Start Building an Email List*

   Offer a discount or freebie in exchange for email addresses

   Use Shopify, Mailchimp, or a landing page tool

3. *Create Your SOPs (Standard Operating Procedures)*

   Document how you do things so others can take over

4. *Hire Help*

   Start with a VA for basic admin tasks

   Gradually delegate marketing, design, or customer service

5. *Explore Other Platforms*

   Claim your brand name on Shopify, Instagram, Facebook, Pinterest

   Set up a basic Shopify store as a brand home

6. *Set Quarterly Goals*

   Revenue targets

   New product launches

   Number of new reviews

   Customer retention or repeat sales

7. *Protect Your Business*

   Consider forming a legal business entity (LLC, Ltd, etc.)

Get business insurance if needed

Track your finances and set aside money for taxes

FINAL WORDS: BECOMING THE CEO

The leap from side hustle to business owner doesn't require a fancy title. It requires a shift in mindset. You are no longer just trying something out. You are building something meaningful, something that creates value for others and freedom for you.

You don't need to have it all figured out today. You just need to take the next smart step.

This is your empire in the making.

Own it.

Let's move forward into building your brand beyond the Amazon marketplace, cultivating loyal customers, and creating a future with your online business that you once only dreamed about.

In the saturated world of online selling, where countless businesses vie for customer attention, having a distinct brand identity is the key to differentiation and long-term success. This chapter delves into the power of branding and equips you to craft a unique brand voice that resonates with your target audience.

Your Branding: More Than Just a Logo

Think beyond just a logo or a catchy slogan. Your brand identity is the essence of your business - the personality that sets you apart from the competition. It's the story you tell, the emotions you evoke, and the promises you make to your customers. A strong brand:

Builds Trust and Credibility: A consistent and well-defined brand identity fosters trust with potential customers, making them feel confident about choosing your products or services.

Creates Customer Loyalty: When customers connect with your brand on an emotional level, they're more likely to become loyal advocates who consistently return for repeat purchases and recommend you to others.

Drives Recognition and Recall: A memorable brand identity makes you stand out in the crowd. Customers will remember your brand name, logo, and overall aesthetic, making it easier for them to find you again in the future.

Example:

Imagine you sell eco-friendly, handmade yoga mats. Your brand identity could be centred around themes of sustainability, wellness, and mindfulness. This would be reflected in your brand name (E.g.,'Tranquil Terra'), logo (E.g., an image of a yoga poses on a leaf background), and messaging that emphasises the use of organic materials and the mindful practices yoga promotes.

DEVELOPING YOUR BRAND IDENTITY: THE FOUNDATION

Crafting a strong brand identity requires introspection and a clear understanding of your core values. Here's how to get started:

Define Your Brand Values: What are the core principles that guide your business decisions? Are you passionate about sustainability, exceptional quality, or affordability? Identifying your values helps shape your brand personality.

Craft a Mission Statement: A concise statement that encapsulates your brand's purpose and what you strive to achieve for your customers. For example, 'Empowering yogis to connect with their inner selves through sustainable and ethically-sourced yoga mats'.

Identify Your Target Customer Persona: Who is your ideal customer? Understanding their demographics, interests, and pain points allows you to tailor your brand messaging and product offerings to resonate with them.

Example:

Building on the eco-friendly yoga mat example, your target customer persona might be a health-conscious individual aged 25-45 who prioritises eco-friendly products and practices yoga for relaxation and stress relief.

Creating a Cohesive Brand Experience: Consistency is Key

Your brand identity shouldn't be confined to just your logo. It's about creating a consistent experience across all touch points where customers interact with your brand. This includes:

Website Design: Your website should reflect your brand's visual identity, using the same colour palette, fonts, and imagery as your logo and marketing materials.

Social Media Presence: Maintain a consistent brand voice and aesthetic across all your social media platforms.

Product Packaging: Your product packaging is a prime opportunity to showcase your brand identity. Use eco-friendly materials that align with your brand values and include design elements that echo your logo and brand message.

Example:

The eco-friendly yoga mat brand would ensure their website has a clean, nature-inspired design with earthy tones and images of people practicing yoga in serene settings. Their social media posts would promote healthy living practices and showcase the eco-friendly aspects of their yoga mats using high-quality photos and engaging captions. The yoga mats themselves would be made from recycled materials and feature the brand's logo subtly incorporated into the design.

Leveraging Storytelling in Your Brand: The Power of Connection

People connect with stories. Incorporate storytelling into your brand marketing to forge a deeper emotional connection with your target audience. Share the story behind your brand, your passion for the products you sell, and how your business makes a positive impact.

Use Customer Testimonials: Showcase real customer stories about how your products have benefited their lives.

Create Engaging Blog Content: Develop blog posts or articles that share valuable information related to your niche and weave your brand story into the narrative.

Craft Compelling Product Descriptions: Don't just list features – tell a story about how your product can solve a customer's problem or enhance their life.

Example:

The yoga mat brand could share the story of the company's founder who, inspired by their love of yoga and environmental consciousness, decided to create a sustainable yoga mat option.

They could share the story of the company's founder who, inspired by their love of yoga and environmental consciousness, decided to create a sustainable yoga mat option. They could feature customer testimonials on their website about how the yoga mats not only provide a comfortable practice surface but also contribute to a sense of doing good for the planet. Blog posts on their website could offer tips on eco-friendly living alongside guides for yoga poses specifically designed for stress relief or relaxation. The brand's product descriptions could go beyond simply mentioning the material and dimensions of the mat. They could tell the story of the eco-friendly materials used, highlighting their sustainable sourcing and the positive environmental impact of choosing a recycled yoga mat. By incorporating storytelling throughout their brand messaging, the company connects with customers on a deeper level, fostering brand loyalty and a sense of community around shared values.

Remember creating a powerful brand identity is a continuous process, not a one-time activity. Your brand may need to evolve as your firm does. However, by devoting time and effort to creating a distinct brand identity that resonates with your target audience, you'll be well on your way to establishing a successful and lasting online business. Remember, your brand is your narrative; tell it with passion, sincerity, and a dedication to the principles that distinguish your firm.

EXERCISE & ACTIONS:

Take some time to consider your brand's principles and what distinguishes your firm.

- ***Create a mission statement that expresses your brand's purpose.***
- ***Develop a target consumer persona to understand who you are selling to.***
- ***Create a brand style guide outlining your logo, color scheme, fonts, and overall visual identity.***
- ***Begin implementing brand narrative into your marketing materials and consumer interactions.***

By taking these steps and constantly improving your brand identity, you'll create a strong online presence that attracts loyal customers and propels your company to long-term success.

PART 4
BUILDING BEYOND AMAZON

CHAPTER 11:
CASE STUDIES - REAL PEOPLE, REAL RESULTS

Have you ever dreamt of turning your passion into profit, building a thriving online business, and becoming your own boss? The world of online selling offers a plethora of opportunities, from crafting unique products to sharing your written voice with the world. This chapter delves into inspiring case studies of successful online sellers across various platforms, infused with my personal insights and experiences as an online selling coach. By examining these real-life examples and incorporating the knowledge gained throughout this guide, you'll be well-equipped to embark on your personalised online selling journey.

Let's dive into the inspiring world of successful online sellers:

Case Studies

Caroline's Eco-Friendly Cleaning Success on Amazon

Main Point: This case study highlights how Caroline, a stay-at-home mum, leveraged product research, high-quality ingredients, and strategic use of Amazon FBA to build a successful online business selling eco-friendly cleaning products.

Identifying a Market Gap: Caroline's journey began with recognising a need in the market – a lack of readily available, eco-friendly cleaning products. This demonstrates the importance of market research in identifying profitable niches.

High-Quality Focus: She didn't simply source generic cleaning supplies. She meticulously researched and sourced high-quality ingredients, emphasising the importance of offering products that meet a specific customer need and stand out from competitors.

Building Her Brand: The case study mentions Caroline creating 'her own brand'. This suggests she took the extra step to establish a recognisable brand identity, potentially with a focus on eco-friendliness and quality.

Amazon FBA as a Growth Engine: By leveraging Amazon FBA, Caroline gained access to Amazon's fulfillment infrastructure, allowing her to scale her business efficiently without needing to manage product storage and shipping herself. This highlights the benefits of utilising available resources on online marketplaces to streamline operations and reach a wider audience.

Key Takeaways:

The case study emphasises three key ingredients for success on online marketplaces like Amazon:

Product Research: Identifying a gap in the market and understanding customer needs is crucial.

High-Quality Offerings: Providing products that are superior or address a specific customer preference can lead to a competitive edge.

Strategic Resource Utilisation: Taking advantage of available resources like FBA can streamline operations and facilitate business growth.

From Hobby Baker to Amazon Success Story

Main Point: This case study explores how Michael, a passionate home baker, transformed his love for baking into a thriving online business selling gourmet cookie mixes on Amazon. Through product development, creative branding, and effective advertising strategies, Michael's story demonstrates the power of combining passion with strategic execution on Amazon.

Identifying a Market Gap: Michael noticed a growing demand for convenient, yet high-quality baking experiences at home. He recognised a gap in the market for gourmet cookie mixes that offered premium ingredients and easy-to-follow instructions. This highlights the importance of identifying customer pain points and unmet needs to develop a compelling product offering.

High-Quality Focus: Michael didn't simply create another cookie mix. He meticulously researched and sourced high-quality ingredients, focusing on unique flavour combinations and premium chocolate chips. This commitment to quality ensured his product stood out from generic store-bought mixes.

Building a Memorable Brand: Michael didn't just sell cookie mixes; he created the 'Bake with Bliss' brand. This catchy name and logo instilled a sense of joy and indulgence, differentiating his product from competitors. This emphasises the importance of developing a brand identity that resonates with your target audience.

Amazon PPC as a Growth Engine: While leveraging Amazon FBA for fulfillment, Michael also implemented targeted Amazon Pay-Per-Click (PPC) advertising campaigns. These campaigns helped him reach a broader audience searching for gourmet baking products on Amazon, driving traffic to his product listing and increasing sales. This highlights the strategic use of paid advertising tools available on Amazon to increase product visibility and brand awareness.

Key Takeaways:

Michael's journey showcases three key ingredients for success on Amazon:

Passion and Market Research: Combining your passion with in-depth market research can lead to a unique and in-demand product offering.

High-Quality Focus: Offering products with a superior taste or experience can attract a loyal customer base.

Strategic Marketing and Advertising: Utilising available marketing tools like Amazon PPC can significantly increase product visibility and drive sales.

The Bookish Entrepreneur - From Thrifting to Thriving on Amazon

Main Point: This case study explores the journey of Emily, a book lover with a keen eye for value, who transformed her passion for secondhand books into a successful Amazon business. By leveraging her knowledge of the market, strategic sourcing techniques, and a customer centric approach, Emily's story exemplifies how to build a thriving online bookselling presence on Amazon.

Identifying a Market Gap: Emily noticed a growing demand for affordable, rare, and collectible used books online. Recognising the limitations of traditional brick-and-mortar used bookstores, she saw an opportunity to offer a wider selection and easier accessibility through Amazon. This highlights the importance of understanding customer buying habits and the limitations of existing sales channels.

High-Quality Curation: Emily didn't simply resell any used book she found. She honed her skills in identifying valuable first editions, collectible hardcovers, and books in pristine condition. This focus on quality curation ensured her listings catered to a specific segment of book buyers on Amazon.

Building Trust Through Customer Service: Understanding the importance of trust in the used book market, Emily meticulously documented the condition of each book providing high-resolution photos and detailed descriptions. She also offered prompt customer service, fostering positive reviews and repeat business. This emphasises the importance of building trust and customer loyalty through transparency and excellent service.

Strategic Sourcing: Emily went beyond typical thrift stores. She expanded her sourcing network to include estate sales, library book sales, and online book auctions. This diversified sourcing strategy allowed her to acquire a wider selection of unique and sought-after books, setting her apart from competitors relying on traditional sources.

Key Takeaways:

Emily's journey underscores three key ingredients for success on Amazon in the used book market:

Market Knowledge & Niche Focus: Understanding customer preferences and identifying a specific niche within used books allows for targeted product selection.

High-Quality Curation: Focusing on valuable and well maintained books attracts collectors and serious book enthusiasts.

Customer-Centric Approach: Building trust through detailed descriptions, excellent service, and a commitment to customer satisfaction fosters repeat business and positive word-of-mouth promotion.

PART 4
BUILDING BEYOND AMAZON

CHAPTER 12:
LESSONS FROM THE TRENCHES

This chapter is about the trenches, the late nights, the failed launches, the moments of self-doubt, and the unexpected wins that make the whole journey worthwhile. It's about the gritty details no one talks about in highlight reels. It's also about what I've seen hundreds of beginners get wrong and how you can sidestep those pitfalls like a seasoned pro.

MY BIGGEST WINS AS A MENTOR:

Let's start with the good stuff.

1. Watching People Quit Their Day Jobs

There's nothing quite like watching a student go from side hustle to full-time business owner. I've seen a mum of three go from making £0 online to over £8,000/month in 12 months selling personalised home decor. I've watched a retired teacher find a second career writing and publishing children's books on Amazon KDP. These wins aren't just numbers they're life changes. They're proof that it works if you work it.

2. Seeing People Build Confidence

Some of my favourite moments as a coach come when people stop saying 'I don't know if I can...' and start saying

'Here's what I'm testing next'. That shift in mindset from fear to experimentation, is the true measure of growth. When you treat this like a learning curve instead of a one-shot deal, your success becomes inevitable.

3. Community Wins

There is nothing more powerful than people sharing wins, helping each other troubleshoot, and celebrating progress. My most successful clients are the ones who show up to live calls, participate in mastermind groups, and stay connected. The power of community is not a bonus, it's the secret weapon.

MY HARDEST MISTAKES

And now the stuff that stings a little more....

1. Launching Products Without Demand

Early in my own Amazon journey, I launched a beautiful, high-quality product that nobody wanted. I was so emotionally attached to the idea, I ignored the numbers. I didn't validate the market, check search volume, or scope out the competition. And I paid the price. That product sat in a warehouse for months, collecting dust and storage fees.

Lesson: The market doesn't care how much you love your idea. It only cares about value. Research, always.

2. Scaling Too Quickly

I've helped people go from £1,000/month to £10,000/month, but I've also watched clients crumble under their own growth. Why? They didn't build the backend first. They had no systems, no inventory controls, no support. Their sales exploded and so did their stress.

Lesson: Build for scale before you need it. Put systems in place early.

3. Hiring the Wrong People

I've rushed the hiring process out of desperation, and every time I did, it came back to bite me. Missed deadlines sloppy work, and brand damage - all because I didn't take the time to find the right fit.

Lesson: Slow down. Hire slow, train well, and always trust your gut.

WHAT BEGINNERS GET WRONG (AND HOW TO FIX IT)

Let me be honest. Most beginners don't fail because of bad products or poor strategy. They fail because of mindset, impatience, or inconsistency. Here are the top five mistakes I see - and how you can avoid them:

1. Trying to Do Everything at Once

They want to sell on Amazon, launch a Shopify store, build a social media following, start a podcast, and write an ebook all in the first month. The result? Burnout and confusion.

Fix: Focus on one platform. One product. One audience. Nail it, then scale it.

2. Copying Instead of Creating

Scrolling TikTok and copying what's trending may bring short-term sales, but it won't build a brand. Real success comes from solving problems, telling stories, and adding real value.

Fix: Get clear on your 'why', and let that guide your content, your products, and your voice.

3. Fearing the First Sale Too Much

They spend months tweaking a logo or designing the perfect packaging but never hit publish. Why? Because they're afraid. Afraid it won't sell. Afraid they'll fail.

Fix: You will fail - and that's okay. Start anyway. Each launch is data.

4. Underestimating the Work Involved

Yes, online selling is flexible. Yes, it can lead to freedom. But it's not 'set it and forget it'. It's real work. It requires energy, learning, and grit.

Fix: Treat it like a business from day one. Block work hours. Invest in learning. Show up.

5. Not Getting Help Sooner

Many beginners think they have to 'earn' the right to get help. They try to piece it all together with free content and YouTube videos.

Fix: Fast-track your progress by joining a program, hiring a coach, or joining a community. Proximity matters.

THE POWER OF COMMUNITY & NETWORKING

I've touched on this, but it needs repeating: You are the average of the five entrepreneurs you talk to most.

Selling online can feel isolating. You're building from behind a screen. You're making decisions in a vacuum. That's a dangerous place to be.

But when you join a mastermind, attend a meetup, or join an accountability group everything changes. You get perspective. You get pushed. You get support.

Some of my clients have found business partners, lifelong friends, and marketing ideas that changed their trajectory, all through community.

Don't underestimate this. Find your people. Stay connected.

Your Personalised Path Forward

Now, let's look at your next steps. This is your opportunity to pause and reflect. Not just on what you've read but what you're building.

Reflection Prompts:

1. ***What have been your biggest mindset shifts since starting this book?***
2. ***What limiting beliefs are you still carrying - and how can you challenge them?***
3. ***What platform will you focus on first?***

4. ***What is one product idea you're excited about?***
5. ***What skill do you need to strengthen next?***
6. ***Who can you reach out to for support or accountability?***

Take some time with these. Write your answers in a journal, type them up, or record them on your phone. Don't just think - commit.

A FINAL WORD FROM THE TRENCHES

You don't need permission to build something great. You don't need fancy gear, a huge following, or perfect branding to begin. You need willingness. You need curiosity. You need courage.

Online selling isn't for everyone but it is for those who are willing to be uncomfortable, to learn as they go, and to keep showing up.

I believe in you because I've seen what's possible. I've watched total beginners turn side hustles into six-figure brands. I've seen quiet creators become confident CEOs.

You're not starting from scratch. You're starting from experience and from here, the only direction is forward.

Let's keep going.

The trenches will challenge you, but they'll also shape you into the business owner you were meant to be.

Let's build your empire.

The above case studies offer a glimpse into the diverse paths to success in online selling. But beyond the specific strategies, each seller's journey embodies valuable lessons that resonate with my own experience guiding aspiring entrepreneurs. Let's delve deeper and explore some key takeaways I've gleaned from both these stories and countless coaching sessions:

1. Niche Down: Become the "Go-To" for Your Tribe

Remember Caroline, the eco-friendly cleaning queen? Her success wasn't just about cleaning products – it was about catering to a specific audience – people who prioritise eco-conscious living. Similarly, in my coaching, I often see individuals with fantastic product ideas struggle because they try to appeal to everyone. My advice? Find your tribe!

For example, I once coached a client named Jessica who loved creating handcrafted dog accessories. Initially, she envisioned a broad audience of pet owners. However, after some market research and soul-searching, we identified a niche – dog owners who spoil their furry friends with luxury items. By focusing on high-quality, unique dog bandanas and collars, Jessica attracted a passionate customer base willing to pay a premium. Her shop thrived because she offered something special to a well-defined audience.

2. The Knowledge Never Stops: Embrace Continuous Learning

The online selling landscape is like a chameleon – constantly changing colors. Michael, the baker extraordinaire, exemplifies this perfectly. He didn't just rely on his baking skills; he actively researched current trends and consumer preferences. This ongoing learning is essential. As your coach, I'll be your partner in this learning journey.

Here's how I translate this into action: Let's say you're selling athletic wear on Amazon. Together, we'll stay updated on the latest fitness trends, analyze competitor strategies, and keep an eye on Amazon's algorithm updates. This ensures your product descriptions, marketing strategies, and overall approach remain relevant and competitive in the ever-evolving online marketplace.

3. *Building Bridges, Not Walls:The Power of Community*

Emily, the book whisperer, didn't just list dusty old paperbacks. She actively engaged with her customers, building trust and loyalty through transparent communication and excellent service. This highlights the power of community in online selling. Remember, it's not just about transactions - it's about connecting with people who share your passion.

Here's how I encourage community building for my clients: We can explore creating a Facebook group for your target audience. This space allows you to share valuable content, answer questions, and build relationships with potential customers before they even reach your online store. Additionally, promoting customer reviews and actively responding to feedback shows you care about their experience, further strengthening your online community.

4. *Your Journey, Your Roadmap: Personalisation is Key*

These case studies are fantastic examples, but it's crucial to remember – there's no one-size-fits-all approach. Building a successful online business requires a personalised strategy tailored to your unique goals, chosen platform, and target audience. This is where my coaching shines.

For instance, if your dream is to sell handmade jewellery on Etsy, the strategies you'll employ will differ from someone selling furniture on a platform like Wayfair. Together, we'll conduct platform-specific research, identify your strengths and weaknesses, and develop a personalised roadmap to online selling success.

Remember, success in online selling requires dedication, a strategic approach, and the willingness to adapt and learn. By drawing from these case studies, my personal coaching experience, and your unique vision, we can navigate the world of online selling together and turn your entrepreneurial dreams into a thriving reality.

While these case studies and insights provide a foundational understanding, it's crucial to personalise your approach based on your unique goals, chosen platform, and target audience.

Personalising Your Online Selling Journey: Charting Your Course to Success

Building on the provided case studies and my coaching experience, let's now explore how you can personalise your online selling journey.

1. Identifying Your Niche and Building Your Brand:

Self-reflection: What are you passionate about? What skills or knowledge do you possess that can be translated into a valuable product or service?

Market research: Analyse existing competition within your chosen niche. Identify any gaps or areas where you can offer a unique selling proposition.

Branding: Craft a brand identity that resonates with your target audience and reflects the essence of your offerings.

2. Selecting the Right Platform:

Consider your product/service: Different platforms cater to specific product categories and audiences. Research and choose a platform that aligns well with your niche and target market. (E.g.,, Amazon for physical products, Etsy for handmade goods, KDP for self-published books)

Platform fees and functionalities: Compare the fees associated with each platform and explore the functionalities they offer, such as marketing tools, analytics, and fulfillment options.

3. Crafting a Winning Strategy:

Product optimisation: Ensure your product listings or book descriptions are clear, concise, and packed with relevant keywords to enhance discoverability on your chosen platform.

Pricing strategy: Research your competitors' pricing and establish a pricing structure that factors in production costs, platform fees, and your desired profit margin.

Marketing and promotion: Utilise the platform's marketing tools, explore social media marketing strategies, and consider collaborating with other sellers or influencers within your niche.

My Coaching Insights:

Embrace experimentation: Don't be afraid to experiment with different marketing strategies and track your results. Analyse what works well for your audience and continuously refine your approach.

Content is king: Regularly create valuable content related to your niche. This could include blog posts, social media content, engaging product descriptions, or even informative videos.

Customer service is paramount: Provide exceptional customer service to build trust and loyalty. Respond promptly to inquiries, address any issues efficiently, and actively seek customer feedback to improve your offerings.

Additional Resources and Tools:

Platform-specific resources: Most online selling platforms offer comprehensive guides, tutorials, and seller support resources. Utilise these materials to gain a deeper understanding of the platform's functionalities and best practices.

Online courses and communities: Several online courses and communities cater to aspiring online sellers. These resources offer valuable insights, practical strategies, and opportunities to connect with other entrepreneurs.

Industry blogs and publications: Stay updated on the latest trends and insights within your chosen niche by following relevant industry blogs and publications.

The key to success in online selling lies in adaptability, continuous learning, and a commitment to providing exceptional value to your target audience.

CONGRATULATIONS! YOU'VE REACHED THE FINISH LINE

Welcome back! You can't sell on Amazon, as you recall, and we embarked on a journey together to explore the exciting world of online selling to make sure you can! Throughout this book, we've delved into the foundations of building a successful online business, mastered the intricacies of selling on Amazon.

As a seasoned online selling coach with 10 years of experience guiding aspiring entrepreneurs, I've witnessed firsthand the transformative power of leveraging the online marketplace. This guide has equipped you with the essential knowledge and tools to navigate this exciting yet challenging landscape.

This concludes your exciting online selling adventure! We've traversed a vast landscape together, laying the groundwork for your online business success. Throughout these chapters, you've gained invaluable knowledge and tools to navigate the ever-evolving world of online sales. As a seasoned coach with a decade of witnessing aspiring entrepreneurs flourish in this space, I can confidently say the possibilities are truly boundless.

A Recap of Our Exploration:

Building a Strong Foundation: We embarked on our journey by understanding the booming online sales landscape. We explored various platforms, identified profitable niches, and honed your market research skills, equipping you to make informed business decisions.

Conquering the Amazon Frontier: We then delved deep into the Amazon marketplace, a platform brimming with possibilities. From mastering account creation to crafting captivating product listings, navigating fulfillment options, and launching effective marketing campaigns, you've gained a comprehensive understanding of how to thrive on this vast digital marketplace.

Remember: The key to unlocking success lies in your unwavering dedication to learning, your ability to adapt to changing trends, and a relentless commitment to providing exceptional value to your target audience.

But this is just the beginning! Part 2 of this series promises an even deeper exploration of the online selling ecosystem. Here's a sneak peek at what awaits you:

Expanding Your Reach: Beyond Amazon: We'll venture beyond the Amazon marketplace, exploring additional platforms like Etsy, eBay, Shopify, TikTok and niche specific options to diversify your online presence and reach a wider audience.

Building a Brand that Stands Out: We'll delve into the power of branding, guiding you through defining your brand identity, crafting a captivating story, and creating a cohesive brand experience across all your platforms.

Building a Sustainable Business: Learn strategies for fostering customer loyalty, mastering the art of customer service, and optimising your operations to build a long-lasting and profitable online business.

Don't let this knowledge simmer take action! Leverage the tools you've acquired, explore the resources mentioned throughout this guide, and most importantly, launch yourself into the exciting world of online selling. Whether your dream is to open an online store, publish a book, or offer unique handmade crafts – the possibilities are limitless! So, stay tuned for my free gifts below, where we equip you with the knowledge and strategies to propel your online selling journey to even greater heights. We established a solid foundation, exploring the booming world of online sales, identifying profitable platforms and niches, and equipping you with market research techniques.

We conquered the Amazon marketplace, mastering account creation, product research strategies, crafting compelling listings, navigating fulfillment options, and launching successful marketing campaigns.

Don't let this journey end here! Utilise the knowledge you've gained, leverage the wealth of available resources mentioned throughout this guide, and most importantly, take action. Launch your online store, publish your book, and actively pursue your online selling dreams. The possibilities are truly limitless!

"The only limit to our success is the limitation of our imagination." - Albert Einstein

This phrase by Albert Einstein wonderfully captures the limitless possibilities that exist in the realm of eCommerce. With a touch of imagination, a strategic approach, and the willingness to learn, you can transform your ideas into a thriving online business.

As a coach, I firmly believe that with dedication and a touch of creativity, you can transform your ideas into a thriving online business. Remember that the only constraint to your success is your own imagination.

Enjoy the journey and embrace the challenges, celebrate the victories, and never stop learning and growing as an online entrepreneur.

This journey doesn't end here. I want to share these next steps for you from me completely to help you on your eCommerce entrepreneurial journey.

I wish you the very best in your online selling endeavour.

ACKNOWLEDGEMENTS

Writing this book has been one of the most challenging, humbling, and rewarding journeys of my life. It wouldn't have been possible without the support, encouragement, and inspiration I received along the way.

To my boys, thank you for being my inspiration, without you I would never have started this journey of eCommerce.

To my family, thank you for your endless patience, understanding, and love. Your belief in me gave me the courage to keep going when the road felt long.

To my friends and fellow entrepreneurs thank you for your feedback, your insight, and the late-night conversations that sparked new ideas and reminded me why this work matters.

Thanks to Howard & Kathryn at Rushfirth Creative for their expertise and help with producing this book.

To the clients, students, and readers who've trusted me to guide them on their eCommerce journey your stories, breakthroughs, and persistence inspired many of the lessons in this book. You are proof that ordinary people can do extraordinary things with the right mindset and tools.

To the online business community, thank you for showing up, sharing generously, and reminding me that success doesn't happen in isolation. Community is the secret sauce.

And finally, to you the reader. Thank you for picking up this book, believing in your potential, and taking that brave first step toward building something of your own. I wrote this for you, and I can't wait to see what you create next.

Here's to freedom, fulfillment, and the future you're building.

ANNA DAVIDSON

REFERENCES:

Agarwal, R., & Agarwal, A. (2020). From Mompreneur to Multimillionaire: How to Build a Global Business Empire on Amazon. [John Wiley & Sons]. Retrieved from https://www.amazon.com/Side-Hustle-Main-Millionaire-Paycheck/dp/074406516X

Steve Weber (2018) Make Money on Amazon: A Guide to Maximizing Profits and Increasing Revenue" [Weber Books}

Scott Voelker (2019).Amazon Selling Blueprint: How to Find and Launch Your First Private-Label Product on Amazon in 90 Days or Less [Independently Published]

Clark, S. (2023). Selling on Amazon: How to Launch and Grow a Private Label Business. [Self-published].

AMZScout Blog: Their detailed guide covers the four-step process for starting an Amazon business, including choosing your business model, product research, finding suppliers, and creating optimized product listings

MarketingScoop: Their beginner's guide emphasizes targeting products with existing demand, using Google Trends, and avoiding head-to-head competition with established brands

MarketingScoop (Additional Ideas): Explore their article on 31 lucrative Amazon business ideas, including retail arbitrage and self-publishing with Amazon KDP

Forbes: An entrepreneur's perspective on why starting an Amazon business can be a smart move, focusing on product optimization and creating your own brand

Amazon Seller Central: Their checklist provides essential steps for starting an ecommerce business in 2024, from understanding what ecommerce entails to scaling your operations

https://www.yourecomagent.com/amazon-fba/the-best-products-to-sell-on-amazon-fba-a-comprehensive-guide-2/

Global Ecommerce Sales Growth Report (2024) - Shopify

How To Sell On Amazon: 2024 Guide – Forbes Advisor

How To Start An Etsy Shop – Forbes Advisor

E-commerce Platforms: How They Compare + How to Choose One | Coursera

How to Choose the Right Products for Amazon Product Research - Your eCom Agent

How to sell on Amazon | A guide for beginners

https://kdp.amazon.com/en_US/help/topic/G202172740

https://www.lulu.com/

https://www.bookdesignmadesimple.com/

Printed in Dunstable, United Kingdom

76522202R00127